JOURNEYS THROUGH AMERICA

JOURNEYS THROUGH AMERICA

Train Journeys through American Landscapes

Francia Turner

Ridyl Publishing
Santa Monica, California,
U.S.A.

For

my Mother, in memory, who encouraged me to look at art as life,

my Father, whose kindness and humanity have always been my inspiration,

my children, Riga and Dylan, for expecting their Mom to keep up with them,

Mick Bond, President of Colourcraft Printing, for his professional expertise
and quest for excellence in all work that he undertakes,

Dr. Pamela MacKinnon, scientist, author, and educator, for guiding, with her
strength and compassion, thousands of her students and friends,

Lloyd Ehrenberg, artist and musician, in memory, for his irrepressible spirit,
against all physical odds,

and a special debt of thanks to all the staff of Amtrak and Holiday Inn
Worldwide and its franchised hotels, who have cheered me on, looked
after me, and watched out for me, throughout the nearly three years
it took to turn my dream into reality.

Library of Congress Catalog Card Number: 96-92694

Turner, Francia
Journeys Through America: Train Journeys Through
American Landscapes

ISBN 1-889736-01-5 Paperback version
ISBN 1-889736-00-7 Hardcover version

Ridyl Publishing
2118 Wilshire Boulevard, Suite 467,
Santa Monica, California 90403, U.S.A.

Printed in the United States of America by
Colourcraft Printing, Inc.
Culver City, California 90232, U.S.A.

CONTENTS

ACKNOWLEDGEMENTS

My family, for their love and generous support; Sue Martin, friend and colleague, whose warmth and intelligence inspires all who work with her; the men and women of Colourcraft Printing, Inc., for their expertise in the production of this book; Dave Doughty, for his careful coordination of printing processes; Paul Cassidy, for his technical knowledge, assuring the accuracy of reproduction of the pastel paintings; Frank Nickels, for his thoughtful information; Gary Victor, for his multifaceted photographic skills.

Clifford Black, for his encouragement and deep understanding of the work; Mary Anne Reynolds, for her role as a vital link with the media; Dawn Soper, for her considerate organization of special events; Bruce Heard, for his conscientious guidance with the accuracy of geographical information; Lynn Erskine, for writing with enthusiasm and interest about the project.

Hanns Eckert, Gunther Hatt, Anthony Lovoy, Stuart Newmark, and Michael Silberstein, for their continuous involvement in ensuring me essential accommodation; Nelson Zager, who has acted as mentor, and consistently offered me guidance, support, and friendship; Luann Domschke, Los Angeles, and Vilma Belle, Washington, D.C., for their patient coordination of my hotel arrangements in these areas; Patricia Kelly, for her detailed organization of my itineraries; the restaurant "America," Union Station, Washington, D.C., for their valued participation in the book launch.

Dr. Murray C. Clarke, for his specialized knowledge in the field of preventative medicine; and his colleagues, Dr. Geoffrey R. Pfeifer, Phyllis Kaplan, and Danielle Garcia; Jane Kagon and Ed Greenberg, who have given me their friendship and counsel; Avery and Betsy Krut, whose informed interest has been of great help to me; My son, Dylan, for his dedicated work using computer and editorial skills.

A special thanks to the officials based in San Luis Obispo, California, who gave me new perspectives on the importance of the railroad: Senator Jack O'Connell, Eighteenth Senatorial District, California Legislature; The Honorable Tom Bordonaro, Assemblyman, Thirty-Third Assembly District, California Legislature; Laurence Laurent, County Supervisor, San Luis Obispo County; Allen Settle, Mayor of San Luis Obispo; Arnold Jonas, Director of the Community Development Department, City of San Luis Obispo; Dr. Edwin Denton, Superintendent, San Luis Coastal Unified School District; Peter Rogers, Associate Transportation Planner, San Luis Obispo Council of Governments.

AMTRAK

From Amtrak executive offices to train platforms, many employees gave me their friendship and invaluable assistance. I want to especially thank the following Amtrak Executives: Thomas Downs, Chairman, President, and Chief Executive Officer, who shared his love of railroading; Anne Hoey, Vice President, Corporate Management; Robert VanderClute, Vice President of Operations. The book could not have been produced without the coordination of the Public Affairs Department: Clifford Black, Director, Public Affairs; Mary Anne Reynolds, Director, Travel and Consumer Media Relations; Steven Taubenkibel, Media Relations Officer; and Louise Harley, Senior Secretary. I also want to thank other Washington Amtrak employees: Amy Elsbree, Director, Government Affairs; Hope Wood, Executive Assistant to the President; Peggy Gold, Senior Secretary; and the Operations Department.

Each of Amtrak's Business Units were of immense help to me. In the **Northeast Corridor**: George Warrington, President; Barbara Richardson, Chief of Staff and Vice President, Marketing and Communications; Stan Bagley, Vice President of Operations; Richard Remington, Manager of Media Relations; Dave Nichols, Superintendent, Centralized Electrification Traffic Control; Don Knapik, Director, High Speed Rail; Diana Cabot, Director, Vermont Marketing Services; Dave Smith, Service Manager; Susan Winerip, Secretary; Bill Gatchel, Secretary.

In **Amtrak Intercity**: Mark Cane, President; Debbie Hare, Senior Director, Government and Public Affairs; Lee Bullock, Vice President, Customer Service; John Wall, Product Line Manager, Southwest Chief; as well as Ray Lang, Government Affairs Officer; Martha Eannace, Staff Assistant to Vice President, Customer Service; Sheila Smith, Secretary; Karen Thurmon, Secretary; Rhonda Henderson, Secretary; Carol Mosevich, Secretary.

In **Amtrak West**: Gilbert Mallery, President; Dawn Soper, Director, Communications and Public Affairs; Brian Rosenwald, General Manager, Coast Starlight; as well as Jill Moyer, Manager of Finance; Jack Wilson, Product Line Manager, San Diegan; Bruce Heard, Amtrak West Film Coordinator; Dominick Albano, Manager, Public Affairs; Kelli Tharpe, Communications Assistant; Judy Bazan, Secretary, Coast Starlight; and my special thanks to Roy Petrie, Engineer; Thomas Del La Rosa, Engineer; and Phil Gosney, Engineer.

HOLIDAY INN

From the outset of our association, the staff of Holiday Inn Worldwide and its franchised hotels have been most helpful and generous with their hospitality, excited about the project, and have proven themselves to be a caring organization. I want to acknowledge and thank the following: Brian Langton, Chairman, Holiday Inn Worldwide; Craig Hunt, President, The Americas Franchise Division; Michael Silberstein, Director of Operations, North America Crowne Plaza Hotels and Resorts; and for their continual input and contact with the hotels: Craig Smith, Vice President, Public Relations and Communications; and Kerri Wightman, Public Relations Assistant. I also want to thank the staff of individual hotels where I stayed: Terry Biggins, Director of Marketing; Marina Bogrand, Director of Sales; Luann Domschke, Executive Assistant; Pat Hughes, Sales Manager; Terry Kuflik, Director of Public Relations; Mara Lopez-Bernal, Director of Sales; Rene Lopez-Couto, Director of Sales and Marketing; Lorrie Morris, Administrative Assistant; Alan Poston, Assistant Manager; Cindy Rizza, Executive Secretary; Juanita Swallers, Catering Manager; Christine Watson, Executive Manager; Zoe Wong, Executive Secretary.

General Managers and Area Directors

My grateful appreciation goes to the following General Managers and Area Directors who have been of such help to me at every stop on my journeys: Ron Antonucci, Keith Barr, Randall Bohannan, Mark Brennan, Carmen Brun, Edward Buchert, Dennis Burrell, Al Catino, Doug Chipperwa, Ron Clausen, Jeff Cobbledick, Bill Cox, John Culetsu, Fred Della Grotta, Ed Devries, Bob Diduca, Hanns Eckert, Daniel Fevre, Lonnie Field, Edward Foster, Phil Froehlich, Patti Gallagher.

L. Manuel Garza, John Gerstenlauer, Paul Gibbs, Sheila Giovanazzi, Melissa Hall, Gunther Hatt, Hubert Herre, Bruce Hohenstein, Gordon Jackson, Craig Johnson, Tony Johnson, Ghulam Khan, Peter Komar, Tom Kulick, Charles Lagarce.

John Lloyd, Zygmunt Lopuszynski, Anthony Lovoy, Terry Mariano, Mark Mathews, Dennis Miller, Gary Miller, Jack Miller, Randy Money, Rene Neidhard, Stuart Newmark, Kevin Ott, Bob Partlow, Jay Patel, Nick Patel, Michael Payton, Ann Peterson, Tom Poehailos, Moses Qidwai, Kevin Richards, Susan Ridgeway, Jan Rietveld, Rodney Rogers, Ken Scheuering, Craig Schwan, Andrew Schwebel, Larry Scott.

Randy Seifer, John Sherry, Karen Sikora-Berard, John Simonich, Dewaine Smith, William Stanton, Al Stento, Scott Swagler, Craig Schwan, Gerry Temple, Bill Townsend, Scott Uttley, Wauquin Vela, Jim Waldvogel, John Walsh, Al Walters, Lori Walton, David Weiler, Linda Wilcox, Nelson Zager.

PARTICIPATING HOLIDAY INN AND CROWNE PLAZA HOTELS

CROWNE PLAZA HOTEL PHOENIX–Downtown/Civic Center
100 North First Street, Phoenix, AZ 85004

HOLIDAY INN HOTEL TUCSON–City Center
181 West Broadway, Tucson, AZ 85701

HOLIDAY INN SELECT BAKERSFIELD–Convention Center
801 Truxtun Avenue, Bakersfield, CA 93301

HOLIDAY INN HOTEL HOLLYWOOD (Universal Studios Area)
1755 North Highland Avenue, Hollywood, CA 90028

HOLIDAY INN HOTEL LOS ANGELES–City Center
1020 South Figueroa Street, Los Angeles, CA 90015

CROWNE PLAZA HOTEL REDONDO BEACH AND MARINA
300 North Harbor Drive, Redondo Beach, CA 90277

HOLIDAY INN HOTEL TORRANCE
19800 South Vermont Avenue, Torrance, CA 90502

HOLIDAY INN HOTEL WOODLAND HILLS (Warner Center Area)
21101 Ventura Blvd., Woodland Hills, CA 91364

HOLIDAY INN SELECT IRVINE–Orange County Airport
17941 Von Karman Avenue, Irvine, CA 92714

HOLIDAY INN RESORT MONTEREY–Carmel Area
1000 Aguajito Road, Monterey, CA 93940

HOLIDAY INN EXPRESS REDDING
1080 Twin View Blvd., Redding, CA 96003

HOLIDAY INN HOTEL SACRAMENTO I-80 (Northeast)
5321 Date Avenue, Sacramento, CA 95841

HOLIDAY INN HOTEL SACRAMENTO–Capitol Plaza
300 J Street, Sacramento, CA 95814

HOLIDAY INN EXPRESS SALINAS
131 John Street, Salinas, CA 93901

HOLIDAY INN HOTEL SAN DIEGO–On The Bay
1355 North Harbor Drive, San Diego, CA 92101

HOLIDAY INN HOTEL SAN DIEGO–Harbor View
1617 First Avenue, San Diego, CA 92101

HOLIDAY INN SELECT PLEASANTON (San Ramon Area)
11950 Dublin Canyon Road, Pleasanton, CA 95488

HOLIDAY INN HOTEL SAN FRANCISCO–Oakland Bay Bridge
1800 Powell Street, Emeryville, CA 94608

HOLIDAY INN HOTEL SAN FRANCISCO–Civic Center
50 Eighth Street, San Francisco, CA 94103

HOLIDAY INN HOTEL SAN FRANCISCO–Financial District (Chinatown)
750 Kearny Street, San Francisco, CA 94108

HOLIDAY INN HOTEL SAN FRANCISCO–Fisherman's Wharf
1300 Columbus Avenue, San Francisco, CA 94133

HOLIDAY INN SELECT SAN FRANCISCO–Union Square
480 Sutter Street, San Francisco, CA 94108

HOLIDAY INN HOTEL WALNUT CREEK
2730 North Main Street, Walnut Creek, CA 94596

HOLIDAY INN HOTEL SAN JOSE NORTH (Milpitas/Silicon Valley)
777 Bellew Drive, Milpitas, CA 95035

HOLIDAY INN EXPRESS SAN LUIS OBISPO
1800 Monterey Street, San Luis Obispo, CA 93401

HOLIDAY INN HOTEL SANTA BARBARA–Goleta
5650 Calle Real, Goleta, CA 93117

HOLIDAY INN HOTEL STOCKTON
111 East March Lane, Stockton, CA 95207

HOLIDAY INN HOTEL DENVER–Downtown
1450 Glenarm Place, Denver, CO 80202

HOLIDAY INN HOTEL HARTFORD–Downtown/Civic Center
50 Morgan Street, Hartford, CT 06120

HOLIDAY INN HOTEL NEW HAVEN–At Yale University
30 Whalley Avenue, New Haven, CT 06511

HOLIDAY INN SELECT STAMFORD–Downtown
700 Main Street, Stamford, CT 06901

HOLIDAY INN HOTEL WILMINGTON–Downtown
700 King Street, Wilmington, DE 19801

HOLIDAY INN HOTEL WASHINGTON, D.C.–Downtown
1155 14th Street NW, Washington, DC 20005

HOLIDAY INN RESORT NIKKI BIRD (Maingate–Disney World Area)
7300 Irlo Bronson Highway, Kissimmee, FL 34747

CROWNE PLAZA RESORT MIAMI–Newport Pier Beachside
16701 Collins Avenue, Miami Beach, FL 33160

HOLIDAY INN HOTEL ORLANDO ARENA
304 West Colonial Drive, Orlando, FL 32801

HOLIDAY INN SUNSPREE RESORT PALM BEACH–Oceanfront
3700 North Ocean Drive, Singer Island, FL 33404

HOLIDAY INN SELECT TAMPA–Downtown
111 West Fortune Street, Tampa, FL 33602

HOLIDAY INN SELECT ATLANTA–Perimeter Mall
4386 Chamblee Dunwoody Road, Atlanta, GA 30341

HOLIDAY INN SELECT ATLANTA–Decatur (Conference Plaza)
130 Clairemont Avenue, Decatur, GA 30030

CROWNE PLAZA HOTEL RAVINIA (Atlanta's Perimeter Center)
4355 Ashford-Dunwoody Road, Atlanta, GA 30346

HOLIDAY INN HOTEL BOISE–Airport
3300 Vista Avenue, Boise, ID 83705

HOLIDAY INN HOTEL CHICAGO–City Centre
300 East Ohio Street, Chicago, IL 60611

CROWNE PLAZA HOTEL INDIANAPOLIS–Union Station Downtown
123 West Louisiana Street, Indianapolis, IN 46225

CROWNE PLAZA HOTEL NEW ORLEANS–Convention Center Area
333 Poydras Street, New Orleans, LA 70130

HOLIDAY INN HOTEL BALTIMORE–Inner Harbor (Downtown)
301 West Lombard Street, Baltimore, MD 21201

HOLIDAY INN SELECT BOSTON–Government Center
5 Blossom Street, Boston, MA 02114

HOLIDAY INN HOTEL MINNEAPOLIS–Metrodome
1500 Washington Avenue South, Minneapolis, MN 55454

CROWNE PLAZA HOTEL KANSAS CITY, Country Club Plaza
4445 Main Street, Kansas City, MO 64111

CROWNE PLAZA HOTEL LAS VEGAS
4255 South Paradise Road, Las Vegas, NV 89109

HOLIDAY INN HOTEL ALBANY–Turf On Wolf Road (Airport)
205 Wolf Road, Albany NY, 12205

HOLIDAY INN HOTEL BUFFALO–Grand Island
100 Whitehaven Road at East River Road, Grand Island, NY 14072

CROWNE PLAZA HOTEL MANHATTAN
1605 Broadway at 49th Street, New York, NY 10019

HOLIDAY INN HOTEL NIAGARA FALLS–Downtown (At The Falls)
114 Buffalo Avenue, Niagara Falls, NY 14303

HOLIDAY INN EXPRESS STONY BROOK, Long Island
3131 Nesconset Highway, Stony Brook, NY 11720

CROWNE PLAZA HOTEL WHITE PLAINS–Downtown Area
66 Hale Avenue, White Plains, NY 10601

HOLIDAY INN HOTEL YONKERS
125 Tuckahoe Road, Yonkers, NY 10710

CROWNE PLAZA HOTEL COLUMBUS–Downtown
33 Nationwide Blvd., Columbus, OH 43215

CROWNE PLAZA HOTEL PORTLAND–Lake Oswego
14811 Kruse Oaks Blvd., Lake Oswego, OR 97035

HOLIDAY INN HOTEL PORTLAND–Downtown
1021 NE Grand Avenue, Portland, OR 97232

HOLIDAY INN SELECT PHILADELPHIA–City Center
1800 Market Street, Philadelphia, PA 19103

HOLIDAY INN SELECT PITTSBURGH–At University Center
100 Lytton Avenue, Pittsburgh, PA 15213

HOLIDAY INN HOTEL PROVIDENCE–Downtown
21 Atwells Avenue, Providence, RI 02903

CROWNE PLAZA RESORT HILTON HEAD ISLAND
130 Shipyard Drive, Hilton Head, SC 29928

CROWNE PLAZA HOTEL MEMPHIS–Downtown/Convention Center
250 North Main Street, Memphis, TN 38103

HOLIDAY INN HOTEL AUSTIN–Town Lake
20 North I-35, Austin, TX 78701

HOLIDAY INN HOTEL DALLAS–Aristocrat (Historic Downtown)
1933 Main Street, Dallas, TX 75201

CROWNE PLAZA HOTEL HOUSTON–Galleria Area
2222 West Loop South, Houston, TX 77027

HOLIDAY INN HOTEL AND SUITES SAN ANTONIO–Northeast
3855 IH-35 North, San Antonio, TX 78219

HOLIDAY INN HOTEL SAN ANTONIO–Downtown
318 West Durango Blvd., San Antonio, TX 78204

HOLIDAY INN HOTEL SAN ANTONIO–Riverwalk
217 St. Mary's Street, San Antonio, TX 78205

HOLIDAY INN HOTEL SALT LAKE CITY–Airport
1659 West North Temple, Salt Lake City, UT 84116

HOLIDAY INN HOTEL BURLINGTON
1068 Williston Road, South Burlington, VT 05403

HOLIDAY INN HOTEL RUTLAND–Center of Vermont Complex
411 South Main Street, Rt. 7, Rutland, VT 05701

HOLIDAY INN HOTEL WATERBURY–Stowe (Ben & Jerry's)
At Exit 10 - I-89 & Rt. 100 N., Waterbury, VT 05676

HOLIDAY INN HOTEL WHITE RIVER JUNCTION
Holiday Drive & Sykes Avenue, White River Junction, VT 05001

HOLIDAY INN EXPRESS BELLINGHAM
4160 Guide Meridian, Bellingham, WA 98226

CROWNE PLAZA HOTEL SEATTLE–Downtown
1113 6th Avenue, Seattle, WA 98101

HOLIDAY INN EXPRESS SPOKANE–Downtown
801 North Division Street, Spokane, WA 99202

HOLIDAY INN EXPRESS SPOKANE–Valley
9220 East Mission, Spokane, WA 99206

FOREWORD

One of Amtrak's strongest selling points is that from a train window you can see America from a different perspective. Instead of homogenized green highway signs, you glimpse an array of changing sights accessible only by rail. Instead of showing you a blanket of clouds we usher you into the nation's back yard, its canyons and peaks, its seascapes and prairies, its small towns and city skylines, and its gritty industrial soul. Many would say you also see into the American past.

It's not lost on us at Amtrak that "the railroad built this country and opened up the West." That commonly repeated refrain is no myth, but it has taken on mythological proportions. The story of railroad development and growth is part of our national heritage, an archive of the energy and vision invested by our forebears. Few third- or fourth-generation Americans can't lay claim to at least one relative who worked for "the railroad."

For Amtrak's customers and potential customers, this link with the past is imbued with the pleasant pull of nostalgia. For many of those rail passengers, particularly on long distance routes where flying would be faster, taking the train is a chance for a contemplative retreat from the pressures of late-twentieth-century life. If that is the respite offered us by nostalgia, so be it. We unabashedly embrace that built-in marketing tool. But there are other reasons for taking the train, too.

Today we are too often dazzled by communications technology that catapults us through space and time only to arrive at a bewildering array of electronic icons. As we hurtle toward the millennium, we are nearly overwhelmed with information, news, music, opinion, and art. We barely have time to be selective. We seem to be pursued by an urgency to know it all. The logical sequence and comprehensible pace of the view from a train window is reassuring evidence that nature's splendor remains to inspire us. Amtrak can take you away from the stress that seems to overlay our lives.

Francia Turner's *Journeys Through America: Train Journeys through American Landscapes* gives us a special perspective on one of the fundamental advantages of rail travel. More than just views from a train window, her pastel paintings and poetic text convey some of that ineffable sense of kinship with our country — both its past and present — that Amtrak can provide, whether it's a high speed dash on a *Metroliner* or a leisurely rail cruise through the heartland.

But Amtrak and *Journeys Through America* also ring with promise for the future. The railroad makes fewer demands on the environment than any other mode of transportation, and trains are a solution to immobilizing gridlock that threatens our nation's progress. Francia Turner's words and pictures record what we have seen from our train windows and remind us what a treasured synergy exists between train and land. America is a fascinating landscape. Let us both take you there.

Thomas M. Downs
Chairman, President, and Chief Executive Officer
The National Railroad Passenger Corporation (Amtrak)

INTRODUCTION

Journeys Through America is a celebration of the beauty of the United States as seen by rail travel. It has taken nearly three years to complete, during which time I was able to cover over half a million miles of track. This is the first in a series of books written and painted on Amtrak trains and contains twelve of the major routes in its extensive network across the country.

On January 10th, 1983, while living in England, I embarked on my first journey making drawings from a moving train. That day was the beginning of a lifetime partnership with the most romantic vehicle in the world. It is indelibly engraved in my memory because as a birthday present my son had given me a small drawing pad, a set of six pencils, a pencil sharpener, and an eraser to be used for the specific purpose of drawing from the mobile window.

This had been a dream of mine long before actually commencing the project. Every time I had boarded a train and seen the extraordinary panorama of the countryside passing before my eyes, I had been filled with enthusiasm to express this beauty in my work.

As an art student, in addition to all other courses, I studied drawing intensively for twenty-five hours per week. Throughout my career the natural world had been a predominant theme, and I began to translate the skill of quick observation, which gradually enabled me to capture the essence of the landscape.

After more than a year of working in only black, white, and grays, I felt confident enough to add color to my pictures. Monochromatic tones allowed me to focus on the structure of each piece, but color added another dimension and was more difficult to assimilate in a speeding glimpse than the actual form.

By 1986 I had produced a large series of "Pictures from the Train," and had held a number of exhibitions. The Tourist Boards of England, Scotland, and Wales took an active interest in my work and British Rail became my sponsor. It was then that I was able to travel the length and breadth of Britain to complete the book *Journeys: Train Journeys through British Landscapes*, which combined pastel paintings with poetic text about individual areas.

Following its publication I very much wanted to return to America and develop the work on a much larger scale. This was to be my greatest challenge. It was as if all my previous work had been in preparation for the hundreds of thousands of miles I would travel in order to chronicle the landscape of this vast country.

Within the contours of the United States lie a richness and diversity of terrain and geological formations which encompass the shores of two oceans, agricultural plains, far-reaching mountain ranges, canyons, forests, and deserts. Traveling by rail affords the opportunity to see areas which are inaccessible by any other form of land transport. Like a moving hotel, a land cruiser, the train provides an atmosphere for quiet reflection. While sitting comfortably we are able to relax, and are allowed a space where ideas can gel, where we can appreciate the beauty and wonder of scenery which is totally untouched, unique.

When I am painting I look for the prominent features of each scene, some of which are particularly representative of an area, others which are more general but convey a powerful image. Absolute concentration is necessary to create the pictures. As I draw, my hand rarely leaves the paper. My eyes continuously alternate between the momentary view and the page, until I have filled in as much detail as possible before it disappears from my range of vision.

It was soon apparent on the long-distance trains that I would need to ask the attendant to bring breakfast and lunch to my compartment so as not to miss important scenery. Each day I would awake at dawn and work uninterrupted until dusk.

Eventually there were a total of fifteen 18-by-24-inch drawing pads, and over fifty 70-page notebooks of text. Each of the pastel paintings took at least eight journeys to complete, the city skylines requiring more than twenty. On the initial trips, I sketched the outlines, then set up the drawings in sequence to be able to resume work at the relevant locations.

As I paint, the moving landscape affects me deeply, and I am motivated to express these impressions in words. I began writing poetry at the age of fifteen, and, through my children's books which describe aspects of nature, came to merge poetry with factual information. I have always had a keen interest in geography, geology, and archaeology, as well as art, and as I ride on the train these subjects come to life.

I keep a notebook tucked at the side of the seat so that I can immediately write down the thoughts as they come to me. These were transcribed into over a thousand type-written pages, then edited until they formed of a complete chapter for each route, a process which lasted for more than a year.

In all the distances I traveled, no one route stood out more than another. As every state and region has its own particular quality and personality, so does each route. On the train there are no border lines, we see this immense country as one continuous whole. All in nature is interdependent, each element relates to the other, and the train gives this feeling of oneness, a relationship to country soil, the Earth.

While writing the book, the comfort and service provided on Amtrak trains, the well-designed reclining seats in the coach section, and the privacy of the sleeping compartments, enabled me to concentrate fully at all times.

The men and women of Amtrak — from reservations to station and onboard staff — were always kind, with a generosity of spirit and sense of humor. I saw smiles, helping hands, good natured conversation, and a genuine caring for the well-being of every passenger. I felt secure in the knowledge that highly skilled people were looking after me. Traveling for two or three days on one route, passengers build a rapport with the onboard staff that is unlike any other form of land transportation.

The Department of Public Affairs and administrative staff of Amtrak supported me greatly in arranging itineraries, interviews, and the many details necessary to the development of the book.

The information I received while traveling was also very helpful. On Amtrak Intercity trains I encountered the splendor of the West through the eyes of experienced conductors. In New Mexico the fascinating comments of Native American guides on the *Southwest Chief* brought alive the landmarks and history of each area, archaeological sites of twelfth-century dwellings, and geological formations. I listened intently to the guides from the California State Railroad Museum who accompanied the *California Zephyr* on its route over the Sierra Nevada Range, narrating stories of a young West and its pioneers.

For over two years I lived out of suitcases containing clothing, a fantastic array of vitamins, all of my art materials, a word processor, and office supplies, as well as two filled portfolios. Traveling for weeks at a time, I had to be prepared for any changes in climate — winter coats, sweaters, jeans, boots, summer shoes, and blouses. I looked more like a camel than a passenger.

At times riding for two days and two nights, I would arrive at a hotel at midnight, sleep for a few hours, and leave at dawn to catch a connecting train. On other routes I would have a one or two day stopover, during which time I researched the local area. I was constantly on the go.

The enormity of this task would have been impossible without the generous support of Holiday Inn Worldwide and its franchised hotels who participated in the creation of this book and subsequent book tour.

I received exceptional treatment at all the hotels in which I have had the privilege to stay, forming warm friendships with the managers and staff. It was as if I had one giant family all around the country.

As the world's largest single hotel chain, with over two thousand properties, I knew that there would be a Holiday Inn or Crowne Plaza hotel in the towns and cities where I would be stopping, and that I would be assured of the excellent quality of rooms and service synonymous with this name. I respect Holiday Inn's progressive approach to hotel management, including being the first hotel chain to allow children free accommodation with their parents, and their implementation of comprehensive environmental policies.

As an artist who sees and wants to preserve the beauty of the landscape, I am aware that the train, by its efficient use of land and natural resources, is beneficial to the environment, and in some areas is the only form of public transportation. Thousands of people rely on its consistent service for commuting and long-distance travel.

The train provides room in which to rest and work. For me, it is an ideal studio; for many people, as I have frequently seen, it is a place in which to write reports and even hold formal meetings. An example of this in Amtrak's Northeast Corridor is the *Metroliner*, a fast, spacious, reliable mobile office which carries its passengers to and from the centers of major cities between Washington, D.C., and New York City.

The train is also endowed with a distinctive social atmosphere. People are able to walk freely to the dining, lounge, and observation cars, where they can get to know fellow passengers and make new friends. In the evening on long-distance trains, I would eat in the dining car. Many routes now incorporate regional menus, and I was able to taste the diversity of cuisine characterizing the areas through which the train was passing. As a passenger traveling alone, I would always be seated with three people I had never met. By the end of the meal we would be engrossed in conversation.

I have spoken to many passengers who have used and appreciated the excellent facilities which are provided for people with physical disabilities. On long-distance trains there are sleeping accommodations with all the amenities for ease of travel. Passengers with wheel chairs and other requirements can use specially designed coach seating areas and receive assistance from attendants who will also bring meals from the lounge and dining cars.

A highlight of my travels on the West Coast was to experience the revival of an old tradition in American railroading. In May 1995, Amtrak West introduced the Pacific Parlor Car to its *Coast Starlight* service, a graciously refurbished 1950's observation car, available to passengers in the sleeping section of the train. Innovations are featured on a weekly basis; afternoon fruit, wine, and cheese are served. There is a library, games and videos, and candles on the tables to enjoy the evening in an atmospheric setting. The comforts of a cruise ship with the amazing beauty of America's spectacular scenery rolling by at every turn.

One of the most memorable events of my life was being permitted to ride in the engine of the *Coast Starlight* in California from Los Angeles to San Luis Obispo. So as not to distract the engineers, I was accompanied by a supervisor who explained every complex procedure involved in driving the train. I became very conscious of how much commitment engineers make each time they get behind the controls. They must know every inch of track and the surrounding land, as well as being alert to signaling instructions. This is a position of true dedication. I greatly admire their strength and responsibility.

The railroad is a major force in the transportation systems of many countries throughout the world. Commuters arrive with ease into the centers of principal cities. Parents often use the train to take their children on vacations and family outings. The civilized, relaxed style of rail travel is a way of life for millions of people.

For many of the visitors who come to America each year, the train is a natural choice for a tour across the enormous distances of the United States. I have met people from other nations who have praised the service and the images of a life-time that they will take back to their countries as permanent impressions and memories of their stay here. Of the many Americans I met, some were traveling by train for the first time. They had been exhilarated by what they had seen, and said that they would return on their next vacation opportunity, encouraging their friends to accompany them.

The employees of Amtrak have a common bond. They love trains and want their passengers to feel the same way. They are aware of the importance of the history of the railroad in this country, and with innovative practices are paving the way for a strong future in the twenty-first century.

On Christmas Eve, 1994, I went to Niagara Falls on the *Empire Service*. Snow was falling and the countryside was hushed, covered in a silken white blanket. The conductors had been particularly cheerful, and we were all traveling on a day when many people try to arrive home early to be with their families.

As darkness descended and a bright glow could be seen over the peaceful farmlands of upstate New York, I looked up from my notebook to hear a familiar melody being played. The train's whistle was piping out "Jingle Bells." The passengers at first smiled, then chuckled, then laughed outright and clapped, and then started to sing. The engineer continued to play the tune as we traveled into the evening.

It is the train's ability to stir emotions and bring enjoyment to people of all ages that inspires me each day I embark on a new journey. I will always anticipate with wonder the changes that occur in the landscape: the sun reflecting on Pacific waters and Vermont mountains, the dramatic velvet gray of an approaching storm, the soft movement of Western desert sands, and the exquisite lace patterns of Spanish moss on Southern live oak and cypress.

So now sit back, relax, and let your imagination take you to the four corners of these magnificent United States. Feel the motion of the train. Look from the windows and see the cities, small towns, fields, lakes, mountains, and forests passing by, and join with me on my *Journeys Through America*.

F.T.
January 1997

METROLINER, NORTHEASTDIRECT

Leaving Washington, D.C.,
on the *Metroliner*,
through pink cherry blossoms,
the Nation's Capital
opens its doors to spring,
relying on the natural
turn of events in the city
and in the country.
Nature's demonstration,
its clocks set for the new season.

Regeneration, rebirth,
an orientation to optimism.
Winter is on the decline,
summer has yet to come.
Spring, like a young child
learning to walk,
filled with bravado,
creates its colorful display.

Commanding the power
that youth possesses,
the metabolic rate soars
in every pore and blood vessel
of a nurtured Earth.
Sun accentuates rose
and olive-green buds unfurling.
An anthem of color
yet to be composed.

As the train embarks
on its journey north,
blossoms continue
to arrest the eye.

To New Carrollton
and Baltimore-Washington
International Airport,
into the Maryland countryside.

Woodlands reach to the track,
the train is enclosed, embraced by forest,
until suburbs and factories again
claim attention on the approach
to Baltimore, Maryland,
birthplace of the National Anthem.

Seen on the distant skyline,
the world renowned
Johns Hopkins Hospital.

Red brick in the afternoon sun,
insulated, terraced houses
with painted porches,
front and back.

Baltimore brick,
manufacturing,
compressed clay, baked,
forming the city's industrial backbone,
with goods shipped to all corners.

The new Inner Harbor complex
brings a thriving
community atmosphere to the city.
People congregate by its ferry moorings,
adjacent to museums, elegant stores,
and restaurants.

Views across the water to Fells Point,
the picturesque district
filled with restored charm.

From Pennsylvania Station, Baltimore,
impressive stone church spires,
bell towers, high rise offices,
and sculpted monuments to art and history.
Reflections in white on the Susquehanna River
blend into view.

Houses adjoin
weathered timber jetties.
Sailboats navigate
on brisk, flowing waters.

Pebbled beaches,
small yachts becalmed
on hazel-gray moored flats.
Remnants of harbor pilings
project at low tide,
sand and silt interweave.

Then farmlands created
of wheat and corn
take precedence
along the Susquehanna.
Hillsides in the distance
are warmed in the glow
of a near primary palette.
Orange, blue and yellow gleam.

Freight cars group together
in sidings, building their
reserves.

The Delaware River
now dominates the landscape.
Quaint villages take their place
along the shoreline.
Quiet inlets
protect coastal towns
imbued with a feeling
of well-being,
along Chesapeake Bay.

Towns on the river's edge,
wide front porches
on pastel-painted wooden houses,
preserved from the early
twentieth century.
Verandas with swings,
armchairs awaiting evening sitters
are enclosed in screened
seclusion.

To spend a mild evening
in discussion,
or recline, listening
to the sounds of dusk
and the occasional
night train's reminiscent
and familiar whistle.
The train creates
its regular rhythm,
keeps its canter,
tempo, its sustained beat.

Crossing the Gunpowder River,
from Aberdeen
to Havre de Grace,
with views of geometric,
symmetrical, semicircular bridges,
across the Susquehanna,
to Perryville, Maryland.

White timber houses and churches,
yachts and sailing vessels
lapping the smooth waters
of its silent shores.

Into soft and thickly wooded country,
movements of a serene landscape.
Homes along the rail line,
surrounded by new lawns
and gardens without borders
reaching the track.
Village streets
with wide grass verges.
Gentle country towns.

To Delaware's boundary
at Newark, the historic
Mason and Dixon Line,
through lands endowed
with streams and farms,
leading to garden suburbs,
small, sheltered pockets,
hidden, cozy,
behind deep hedges.

Houses built on the outskirts,
filling, spreading towards
the red-brick arched station
at Wilmington, Delaware.

This thriving port
of the Brandywine River Valley,
seventeenth-century
colonial settlement,
growing to lead the world
in chemical development.

Passing river barges
along the Delaware,
where sea birds wade
and seek sustenance
from sands at low tide.

Fuel tankers mingle
with tugboats,
and seaport cranes
shift earthly cargo.
Factories line,
and industry succeeds,
to the shore.

From Wilmington,
houses, terraced and detached,
two and three story,
timber primed in tans,
greens and blues,
some turreted,
all distinctive.

Oil refineries,
massive steel works,
stock car yards.
Yellow and deep-terra-cotta
chimney stacks,
fortifying power, electricity pylons,
spherical cylinders containing
oil and gas fuels.
The center of progress
magnified tenfold.

We enter lands, Swedish settlements
of over two hundred years,
approaching New Castle.
Then crossing the border,
with broad views of the Delaware,
to Chester, Pennsylvania.

To Philadelphia,
whose entrance is announced
by colorful boathouses
lining the shore of the Schuylkill River.
Adorned with lights
along each eve and gable,
they add a special atmosphere
to William Penn's
"City of Brotherly Love."

The impressive vision,
eighteenth-century and modern,
whose recent skyscrapers
unify, joining the magnificent
City Hall and buildings in the tradition
of early Pennsylvania,
creating the shape of a city based
on powerful ideas and ideals.

Philadelphia,
artistic and scientific center.
The Philadelphia Museum of Art,
the Franklin Institute,
the Academy of Natural Sciences,
Pennsylvania Academy of the Fine Arts,
the Philadelphia Orchestra.

Known as the evocative
"Cradle of Liberty,"
home of the Liberty Bell
and Independence Hall.
30th Street Station,
hub of the Northeast Corridor,
uplifting spirits,
strength in marbled elegance,
cathedral-like pillars
and epic relief sculptures.

City representing industry,
the great complex
of refineries producing
power and energy,
through its coal, iron and steel.
America's prosperity forged
in the Pennsylvania
of the industrial revolution.

Factory buildings, dye works,
warehouses replete with
manufactured goods.
The mega-strength bordering
onto the Delaware River,
where heavy freighters and cargo vessels
navigate its swift currents.

To Trenton,
state capital of New Jersey,
with its bright, confident sign,
"Trenton Makes — The World Takes,"
as its manufacturing motto.
The glowing emblem to New Jersey's
industrial ethic.

Continuing on, thick hedges lead
to Princeton Junction, at West Windsor,
gateway to Princeton University.
Small firms and houses
protected and enclosed
by full foliage,
shrubs and trees.

Suburban and rural New Jersey,
where woods and farmland become one,
creating a community with mobility
to centers of commerce and trade.

The *Metroliner* passes through
through office-block towns,
to Metropark station.
Green copper
on slate church steeples,
cable wheels and towers.

A forest runs from this
modern business center
to the outskirts
of Newark, New Jersey.
Woodlands have been cleared
through centuries-long development,
but still this natural boundary stands.

Ranch-style homes,
building tracts
settle into the unfolding
countryside.
Screen doors open
to let through the breeze
of late afternoon.

White blossoms frame the track,
then warehouses on the edge
of urban development follow.
Available space,
paintworks,
scrap metal yards,
cast iron bridges
transporting vehicles
up and over the Passaic River.

Apartment houses,
clotheslines,
satellite dishes,
produce carriers,
moving and storage,
jewelry merchants,
gas stations, banks,
and car dealerships add to the flavor
as the city opens its gates, inviting
and incorporating the hum and buzz,
the activity of urban life.

All and more converge,
through and under bridges,
pathways,
water destinations,
to the bustling commercial center
of Newark.

The train now progresses towards
Pennsylvania Station, New York City,
through the engineering feat
of the North River Tunnels,
beneath the broad Hudson,
to the metropolis of the nation.
The monuments to human
power and ingenuity stand firm.
The open and closed case
of a city's story.

A peach glow sweeps across the magnetic
island, with bridges outstretched,
calling and beckoning, to gain entry
to the treasures within its walled fortress,
upwards and beyond.

All this to behold
in an instant's dedicated vision.

The New York skyline
enters on the evening horizon.
Towering superstructures,
monoliths outstanding,
fulfill the city's boundaries.

Lighted buildings,
metropolis landing.
New York,
city of the eastern
Western Hemisphere,
with giant overview
of the Hudson River
and all surrounding
waterways and byways,
highways, throughways.
Always alive with undaunted
excitement.

Home to edifices
and monuments
known in the world's
four corners.
The Empire State Building,
Broadway,
Times Square,
Rockefeller Center and Plaza,
the New York Stock Exchange,
the Metropolitan Museum of Art,
the Museum of Modern Art,
American Museum of Natural History,
Lincoln Center,
the Guggenheim.

The widespread
urban suburbs
of the Hudson.
The Brooklyn and
George Washington bridges.
The pieces of the jigsaw
adding up, summing up the whole
of Manhattan Island
and mainland.

Wonderful vantage point.
Every aspect,
all moods
and membranes
of human life
are revealed.

The upturned face
of this vast nation,
this catalyst
of cultures
and passionate beliefs,
New York.

Morning,
on leaving the sky high city,
life comes down to earth.
No longer towers reaching upwards
and onwards into the atmosphere,
expressing light from a thousand
elevated rooftops, conversing
with the universe in bright code,
explaining our presence here.

Heading north
over Hell Gate Bridge,
across Pelham Bay
to New Rochelle,
the *NortheastDirect*
glides through leafy suburbs,
and past the harbors
of Long Island Sound,
as if hundreds of miles away
in spirit
from the exhilaration
of the great city.

Arriving at Stamford,
work in progress,
technology prosperous,
soft Connecticut
tree-lined villages,
giving way to technical works.

Through South Norwalk,
Westport, Southport,
to Bridgeport,
harbor to industry,
Connecticut's gateway,
high-rise factories
and warehouses.

Approaching New Haven,
home of Yale University.
New England, timber plentiful,
homes built from local materials,
painted, some in planks,
some carved shingles.

On the Shore Line route,
extending from New Haven to Boston,
marshland becomes
isolated, sheltered
bays and inlets.
The sea can be seen
like a ribbon
on the horizon line,
with rivers connecting
as it approaches the land.

Atlantic emerging,
with speed and sailboats
displaying their skills.
The Thimble Islands,
miniature outposts
where sea birds nest.
Evergreens shaped by thick
sea winds and mists.
Water lilies, deep-rose
and magnolia,
in marshy headlands.

To Old Saybrook,
quiet woodlands
and occasional houses.
Along Niantic Bay,
following the water's edge
on silvery beaches,
coastal winds gently brush at grasses
dusted with layers of fine sand.

To New London, on the River Thames,
with upright, steepled churches
painted white
in the solid New England style —
simple, Puritan, Pilgrim,
functional.
Sailing boats congregate
in the working harbor.

Ferries transport passengers
to Fisher's Island, Orient Point
and Block Island.

There is a distinctive quality
in New England coastal towns
which preserve their historic
buildings and manner,
giving a sense of grace and permanence.
Mystic and Stonington, Connecticut,
and Westerly, Rhode Island,
all retain their unique individuality,
yet share this common bond.

The route then enters
deciduous forests
towards Kingston,
where houses continue
a tradition elegant in design.

Nearing Providence,
views of Narragansett Bay
are seen from East Greenwich.
Homes with private jetties and lawns,
with picnic chairs and tables,
overlook the sea.
Yachts, small and large,
are moored together
as if in family groups.

The spring harbor makes ready
for the new season's rush.
Imagining waters replete
with fluttering sails,
hot and beautiful
New England summers,
temperate sun,
white heat reviving,
breezes replenishing,
soothing the skin and spirit.

To Providence,
major New England center
of commerce and industry,
whose imposing structure,
the golden-domed State House,
can be seen on approaching
this Rhode Island capital.

Through Massachusetts countryside
to Route 128 station,
on the *NortheastDirect's*
entrance to Back Bay,
and Boston's striking, century-old
marble South Station.

City of history,
of the American Revolution.
Boston, capital of Massachusetts,
honoring its early seventeenth-
and eighteenth-century buildings,
Faneuil Hall, Quincy Market,
the Old State House,
the Old North Church,
the Old South Church,
the House of Paul Revere,
and Bunker Hill Monument.

Boston, on Boston Bay,
seaport, shipyards, waterfronts,
maintains its winding stone-cobbled streets,
its Beacon Hill character and charm.
Red-bricked and shuttered.
Hanging baskets of richly hued
and varied blossoms
add color to the treasured buildings,
remaining as in times past.

Center of education and culture,
Museum of Fine Art, Museum of Science,
and its renowned universities
and colleges.
Its many parks,
the Boston Common,
and the unique swan boats
navigating the pond and rock island
of the beautiful Public Gardens.

Boston,
city of America's birth and growth,
upholding its accomplished past,
and encouraging
its prominent future.

VERMONTER

On its journey southward,
through majestic Vermont's
northernmost station,
St. Albans,
the *Vermonter* crosses
the Lamoille River,
and passes ancient
archaeological remains
at Arrowhead Mountain Lake.

We follow on a quiet,
gentle course,
spring's cool birthplace,
over glistening, frosted
brooks and rock coves.

Snow in mid-April,
Easter snow.
Seasons are not rushed,
they take their time.
Winter does not abandon its niche,
its special place.
It relinquishes its hold
over frost-bound pastures
with great reluctance,
allowing full and complete
hibernation,
permitting the long winter sleep
for creatures and flora.
It fulfills its cycle.

Wildlife stirring, rustling,
preparing in nests and dens,
all experiencing spring's deliverance,
the time to leave their cool dwellings,
their metered environments.

All awaiting.
Buds primed in anticipation
of the sun's persuasive
repositioning.
Caressing the Northern
Hemisphere,
encouraging each tiny leaf
to burst forth
upon this noble state,
of mind and being,
Vermont.

All alive and well,
reconstructing
the metabolism of time.
All remembering
on the age old clock,
the call to face the sun's interrogation,
to be ready when the rays of change
awaken a sleeping Earth,
and begin again
the perennial experiment,
the continuing flow,
the unending current.

Here is a special quality
of air and light.
The beauty of dramatic
mountain landscapes,
of woodlands
boasting an abundance
of famed sugar maple,
waiting to be tapped
and condensed
into sweet nectar.

The elegance of New England
town and country buildings
shines through the windows
of our train, as it makes its way
towards Burlington's station stop,
Essex Junction.

Preserved city.
Distinguished eighteenth-century
university, built of brick and stone,
by the shores of Lake Champlain.
Cool, silver, smoke-blue haze,
reflective clouds of powder gray.

The Green Mountains,
brilliant ivory, pristine slopes,
inclines, sharp escarpments.
Single stone layers to penetrate,
leaving their bronze marks,
their steel inscriptions,
pewter lines, on a clear,
untouched, defined image.

Forests of fir and peaks glowing
challenge the cool
spring light to diminish
their wintry cover.

Streams surge from rushing falls,
snow drifts deepen
on frozen hillsides.
Mobile branches lean
and sway, blanketed,
heavy with layered frost.

Translucent and opaque
spun crystals,
icy to the touch,
form patterns on ash-gray rock,
sea gull stone,
cloaked with glacial film.

Villages with timber houses,
farmsteads, iron red against white.
To Waterbury,
station to the luminous summits,
the dazzling ranges
of the ski region of Stowe.

Through the Winooski River Valley.
Embankments multilayered
with deep flint, maroon
and ocher pigments
shine out in dark contrast
to an earlier blizzard's
iridescent tones.

From Montpelier,
Vermont state capital,
tractors are becalmed
by ice-bound pastures.
All life is on the alert
to the winter's freeze.
Throughout,
farmers have kept their herds
immune to the chill,
producing hardy breeds.

Pine plantations
don newborn saplings
bursting through snow cover,
as the April sun promotes
glittering shadows
on the delicate growth.

To Randolph,
passing through villages
nestled beneath
gleaming hillsides,
we find New England churches,
specialized,
with clear, patterned
steeple windows.

Four-story timber houses,
barn shaped to protect
from sharp and lashing storms,
bear the steep roofs
becoming to a land
where dense snows prolong,
weighing heavy on the essence
and structure of the home.

Mountain rapids,
crushed-velvet rock,
pressed satin-lace,
iced-water crystals.
Hills receding, foreshortening,
to White River Junction.

Silver gulls perch
on polished boulders,
ascend and hover
over the White River.
Swirling flocks, pearl gray,
shimmering and opalescent,
born in the fresh,
pure air of New England,
accompany the train
as it glides towards
the station at Windsor,
approaching the radiant peaks
of Mt. Ascutney.

Lumber mills abundant
in their natural resource
gain access to Claremont,
New Hampshire,
and from here we again
enter Vermont at Bellows Falls.

The train continues
its quiet descent
through forested uplands.
The Green Mountains
now become gentle, flowing hills,
pine and birch covered,
to Brattleboro.

Crossing the broad
Connecticut River,
between frosted fields,
the track steers through
pinewoods,
with only the presence
of these towering trees
on either side.
We are engulfed in the beauty
of April flora and foliage.

Through Northampton,
Massachusetts, snow now subsides
on open hillscapes.
To Amherst,
known for its celebrated
nineteenth-century poets,
and eminent schools and colleges.
A quiet center of culture
amidst farm and pastureland.

Its houses set a scene
from a tranquil time,
some painted,
some primed in stains,
to preserve, yet tint
with a natural glow.
Some shingled,
with broad back gardens,
picnic tables,
and wood piles reduced
through the winter's usage.

Massachusetts towns,
with century-old
red-brick mills, factories,
and construction works.

Small suburbs blending into one.
Timber merchants,
industrial warehouses
and low office buildings,
on the outskirts
of the early trading settlement
and modern manufacturing city,
Springfield, Massachusetts.

Through Windsor Locks, Connecticut,
crossing the canal which bears its name,
and following on a parallel course,
to seventeenth-century Windsor.

We reach the capital
of Connecticut, Hartford,
whose landmark,
the first American State House,
is emblazoned in gold leaf.
Founded by Dutch settlers
in the early Colonial period,
it has become a significant
commercial center,
noted for its museums and parks.

To Berlin, Meriden,
and Wallingford,
where metalworking —
the manufacture
of tin and fine silver —
has been the prime industry
for over two centuries.

Then to New Haven, old presence
of the Connecticut consciousness,
perpetuating through its university
the educational tradition.

Arriving at Bridgeport.
Cranes, ocean going freighters,
and cargo ships.
Marshlands to the sea.
Open harbor,
town houses on the bay,
dove gray, beige,
and pale green.
Subtle colors trimmed
with white.

From Stamford
the *Vermonter* departs through
peaceful Connecticut towns
to New Rochelle, New York.
Traveling over Hell Gate Bridge,
extending from one reality to another,
from one time zone, time frame,
we are transported above and across.
The metropolitan
architectural forms
are ingrained upon our vision,
our points of reference.
The geometric puzzle,
all pieces in place,
New York.

We continue south
through the Northeast's
prominent business,
manufacturing,
and cultural cities.
Newark, Metropark,
and Trenton, New Jersey,
Philadelphia, Pennsylvania,
Wilmington, Delaware,
and Baltimore, Maryland.

The train then stops
at Baltimore-Washington
International Airport
and New Carrollton
on its route to Washington, D.C.

Union Station,
the elegance and grace,
extraordinary renovation,
domed ceilings,
immaculate gold leaf,
mahogany and marble.
Restored to a point
of excellence and beauty
in the heart of the Nation's Capital.

EMPIRE SERVICE

From Niagara Falls, New York,
privileged guardian
of America's largest
and most awe inspiring waterfall,
the *Empire Service* embarks
on its southward journey
to New York City.

Deep summer,
white rapids
of the Niagara River.
Churning movement,
billions of gallons, continuous flow,
of clear, uncompromising
pressure.

Water rushed
to a crashing climax,
over a precipice
allowing no clue to its existence,
until the last dramatic moment,
when suddenly the land escapes
its permeating grasp.

In a thrilling leap,
all is changed.
The quiet world
as is known
becomes a frothing,
overflowing mass
of air and light.

A roaring torrent,
not stopping
for any obstacle in its path,
expressing the power
of a force so great
as to be unchallenged.

From this overwhelming
natural monument,
attracting visitors of every nation,
we follow a course
filled with the exquisite
pastoral beauty of the New York
countryside.

Soon electricity and industry
dependent on the fast flowing
Niagara River are replaced
by farmlands, cattle pasture,
and native flora.

Arriving at Exchange Street Station,
Buffalo, the state's great railroad
and manufacturing city
on the eastern shores
of Lake Erie.

Here commences the route,
over three hundred and fifty miles,
of the Erie Canal.
The significant channel, east to west.
Early nineteenth-century
mule-drawn barge system,
uniting the waters of Lake Erie
and the Mohawk River
to form a major link with
the powerful Hudson River at Albany,
leading to the city of New York.

All ports along its course
developed and prospered,
becoming world leaders
in manufacturing and trade,
creating an unusual contrast
to the quiet rural surroundings.

From Buffalo-Depew station
to Batavia,
where wildflowers,
daisies, thistles,
scarlet berries,
lavender and goldenrod
are intertmixed
with strong standing,
maroon-tipped bull rushes.

Hay in bales,
baked by the August sun,
awaits collection.
Planted fields
surround tractors
in readiness
for a full day's events.

To Rochester,
on the Genesee River,
whose heritage as America's
city of photography
stands out in this industry's
offices and factory buildings.

Beyond its boundaries,
we again reach
a depth of farmland,
a patchwork of fields
in and preparing for
cultivation.

From streams and marshlands,
the Mohawk River flows.
Gentle, almost still.
Reflections of bordering trees,
with growth assured
in this temperate landscape.

Sloping meadow country
entices gulls searching for fish
in tributaries
resplendent with
reed-covered islands.

In the deep heat of summer,
this lush river valley
surprises us with leaves
of early autumn colors.
Outbursts of magenta and dusky rose
become intermediaries between
corn and forest thickets.

Willows sweep and brush
the fertile earth,
and oaks make
their graceful stance.
Cattle gather,
black and white herds,
in country grazing pastures.

Amidst violet, carmine
and fuchsia wildflowers
adorning meadowland,
herons stand majestically
in sheltered ponds,
surrounded by ferns
and deep vegetation,
to Palmyra and Clyde.

Through orchard country
to the city of Syracuse,
known from the seventeenth century
for its vast salt production
from the waters
of Lake Onondaga.

Leaving the commercial
district and passing
its gabled houses,
we again enter
a countryside,
mint condition,
of unclaimed forests.

A mountainous vista now unfolds,
with views to the northern highlands
spreading and stretching
far into the distance.

Laurel and ash,
oak, beech and chestnut
fill the surrounding villages
and single farms,
as the *Empire Service* continues
towards the copper and brass
factories of Rome, New York.

To Utica,
whose distinctive
Children's Museum
can be seen from
the beautifully
restored station
of this prosperous
industrial center.

Through the valley
of the Mohawk,
south of Utica,
we pass racing stables
where owners and trainers
arrive to display
their thoroughbreds.

Corn fills all arable space,
ripe and ready to be picked,
while in the distance,
hills become ever more prominent.

The countryside,
serene, tranquil,
provides the traveler
with a backdrop
for reflection.

A feast for the eye,
a storehouse of memories
of river outings,
fishing trips,
summer vacations,
and we are privileged
to view upstate New York's
inspiring scenery.

Sunday fishermen wave
as the train speeds past.
Families wait at railroad crossings
with little children in their arms,
smiling at the powerful
engines and railroad cars,
responding to the strength,
giving right of way
and recognition.

Steep sided, tree-filled slopes
follow the Mohawk.
This gentle meandering waterway
provides the focus.
Still-glass images
clarify tree reflections.

Wildflowers continue in shades
ranging from deep reds to soft corals.
Farm buildings with silver silos
dominate the surrounding
landscape, and command views
from their modern hill forts.

To Little Falls, St. Johns.
The locks of the Erie Canal
keep the level,
reducing flow, increasing passage
upon its channeled path.

Pastoral scenes,
eighteenth-century landscapes.
Blink, and in an instant,
we return to an earlier time,
to the elegant pillared buildings
seen from the station platform
at Amsterdam, New York.

Approaching the major
industrial city of Schenectady,
electricity and railroad center,
retaining its carefully
restored and conserved
colonial "Stockade District."

We follow the Mohawk
through small
suburban settlements
to the state capital
of New York, Albany.

Seen from the station
at Rensselaer,
the compelling skyline
combines the classical
and ultramodern.
The Capitol, of extraordinary
Italian Renaissance
and Romanesque design,
stands out against the sleek lines
of the Empire State Plaza.

This eminent cultural center
encompasses
the New York State Museum,
the Albany Institute of History and Art,
theaters for the performing arts,
and the stately architecture
of its civic buildings.

From here
the deep Hudson River flows,
spreading its banks beneath
timeless mountain settings
and rippled beaches.

South to Hudson,
picturesque town.
Little islands
almost within reach at low tide.
On one a lighthouse stands alone.

Across the water
the Catskill Mountains
grow swiftly
to full height,
nearing Rhinecliff.
We see tree-covered ridges,
vertical escarpments.

Mansion estates
reside on high ground
leading down to the water's edge,
towards the manufacturing town
of Poughkeepsie.

Beneath hills
casting their blue shadow,
the unexpected
form of Bannerman's Castle
comes into view.
This stronghold appears
as an ancient ruin, replica
reminiscent of a Scottish castle.

Along fern-laden banks
to Cold Spring, we are then drawn
to an impressive stone fortress,
guarding the surrounding
towns and countryside,
the distinguished
West Point Military Academy.

To the early Dutch settlement
of Croton-Harmon.
Passing the small towns
and villages of Tarrytown,
Irvington, Ardsley-on-Hudson.
To Yonkers, comfortable community
within reach of the metropolis.

We glide along
the magnificent Hudson,
where quiet, tree-filled embankments
suddenly become populated,
high-rising structures.
Unforgettable views
of the George Washington Bridge
invite the world to partake
of the magical presence.
The attraction of the city beckons
and the *Empire Service* is propelled
to its heralded destination,
New York.

CAPITOL LIMITED

Leaving Washington, D.C.,
on the *Capitol Limited*,
mid-afternoon, late winter,
through Silver Spring to Rockville.
Intimate landscape,
close proximity,
the still beauty
of the Maryland countryside
is sketched upon our memories.

Lace-like patterns of filtering
sun through shaded branches.
Shapes of permanence, unchanging,
growing into powerful, renewed life forms.

The train's reunion with country earth.
Remnants of winter giving and abandoning,
shedding leaves and bark to the elements,
fertilizing future growth.

We perceive the darkened outlines
of Sugar Loaf Mountain,
following along the shores
of the Potomac River,
crossing into West Virginia.

At the compelling meeting point
of the Shenandoah and the Potomac,
we reach a site of rustic tranquility,
the unforgettable river crossing
to historic Harpers Ferry.

To Martinsburg, West Virginia,
and Cumberland, Maryland.
At dusk the train commences its ascent
into the Allegheny Mountains.
Forging up arduous grades,
climbing with veritable power,
it attains the summit at Sand Patch.

On the descent, we quietly follow
the curving route to Connellsville,
through coal mining country,
to Pennsylvania's
world leader in steel, Pittsburgh.
The incandescent lights
of working mills accompany
our midnight voyage.

We pass Alliance, Ohio,
towards the state's largest city,
the influential port of Cleveland,
and the nearby town of Elyria.

Awakening as the train
reaches the major
glass producing center,
Toledo.
Snow had fallen
throughout the night,
a light cover glistening
on winter-hardened soil.

Farms and villages blend together,
gilded-tan straw remaining
above the delicate snow cover.
Mint-green lawns emerge
through an icy film.

A deep calm, the peaceful hush
of a land immobile, fused into one
by the incongruous combination
of frozen particles,
crystallized, solidified,
which on view
make a distant landscape
appear as soft as lamb's wool,
as quiet as the moment
just before dawn.

Snow turns this
widespread Indiana farmland
into a magic plain.

Sun encourages
shadowed highlights,
and passing through unpaved
small towns,
a scrap yard,
with twisted heaps
of metal rusting,
becomes a gallery
of winter sculptures.
Jagged triangles, spiked forms
push through, reaching
into the luminous pearl sky
from white, air-spun linear
prisms.

Giant wooden spools
of electric cable emptied
of their precious cargo
lie transformed
amidst dried timber,
approaching Waterloo, Indiana.

Tractors, Caterpillars,
plows, snowplows,
building equipment, steam rollers,
all lightly embellished,
preened and beautified
by the chilling natural phenomenon.

Miles of farmland with settlements,
scattered developments, new homes
built on now crisp, tinted-white fields,
complete with satellite dishes
bringing the world
to outstretched towns
throughout America's heartland.

A golden Shetland pony
searches for tender shoots
near clumps of trees left standing.

These form copses, shields,
stalwart protectors
of pine plantation groves
and frost-bound straw remnants
of autumn's ripe harvest.

Grain silos shine, domes gleaming
through the haze of the winter sun.
Plowed soil, furrows shaded
in deep earth tones and white,
row upon row,
leading to distant fields
of winter wheat,
on the outskirts
of Elkhart, Indiana.

Past ice-bound paddocks,
diamond studded.
Crystal-coated corrals
glimmering, glittering,
a radiant jeweled array.
Red barns with corrugated
ivory roofs spark brilliance
to this monochromatic display.

And then,
as if out of nowhere,
five deer, light in their winter coats,
leap across a pristine field.
They had been grazing
through snow-tipped grasses
until the silent country
was alerted to the train's
oncoming motion.

Waterfowl take flight
from frozen, ice-filled lakes.
Rows of fuel tanks immersed in snow
await the call to their farmer's needs.

On glazed forest floors,
branches create
scattered patterns
on hardened earth.

Past South Bend, Indiana,
the land changes, farmland contours.
Giant grain silos adjoin the track.
Timber yards, small villages,
and isolated farms
reside on gentle slopes.

The early sun rises higher
in a cobalt sky,
melting the superficial layer.
Patches appear, jade mosaics
on cleared ground.

The train passes through
rich, open farm country.
Morning light heightens
the glow of soft tones
on fresh seedlings.
Hedges, rows of full,
lush growth,
act as protecting windbreaks
for ripe Indiana fields.

We pass through
low-lying woodlands,
soft in new buds.
Clear, dark pools.
Regenerated land reaching out
towards the west.

Then suddenly an industrial
complex appears.
Steelworks,
manufacturing giants,
bring the larger community
to the northern farmlands.

A golf course,
bright in new green cover,
leads to Whiting Park
at Hammond-Whiting, Indiana,
with its lake-shore jetty
and sailing boats moored,
secured in a safe harbor.

Within a few moments
the *Capitol Limited* crosses
into Illinois, and the skyline
of Chicago's central hub emerges.

A chrome-steepled church gleams,
shines in the March sun,
attracting its congregation.
Brick and timber houses,
three levels, split-level,
one partially below ground,
made for winters when snows
and winds contain the central North.

And now offices,
factory buildings in the distance.
Cranes, metallic recycling,
city streets and sidewalks.

The older neighborhoods,
suburban single-family homes
built from the 1920's onwards.

Supermarkets and playing fields,
freeways and avenues
created to serve the growing work force.

We see changes in property ownership
and types of construction.
A city renewed several times over,
with archaeological remains
from this century, in tact, preserved.

Then approaching the center,
apartments tower over
urban development.

Comiskey Park,
home of the White Sox,
stands proud as we reach
our destination,
the high rising star
of the Midwest,
Chicago.

SILVER METEOR

From Washington, D.C.,
the Nation's Capital,
George Washington's design
for the shape of government to follow.
A city of national monuments and pride.
The Capitol,
seat of government,
home of democracy.
The White House,
Houses of Congress,
Washington Monument,
the Lincoln Memorial.
Collections of fascination and beauty
at the Smithsonian Institution's
numerous museums
and National Gallery of Art.
John F. Kennedy Center for the Performing Arts.
The National Mall, lined with parks, and buildings
of government, art and science.

Union Station,
the heartbeat, crescendo,
atmospheric beginning
to a voyage
through Southern climes.

Trees of evening,
night departure.
Crossing the Potomac River
we pass the brightly lit,
modern skyline
of Crystal City, Virginia.

The *Silver Meteor*
travels south through cities
pivotal to the development
of the United States,
sustaining a living history,
the continuing lesson.

They share their stories as we ride
through their streets and avenues.
The harmonious architecture endures,
making lasting impressions,
the preservation and conservation
of the birth and infancy
of this great country.

Old Town Alexandria,
Fredericksburg,
then Richmond,
for over two hundred years
state capital of Virginia.
All instrumental
in the American Revolution.

In these, and the influential
coastal cities of the South,
we can go back in time
through their efforts
to keep this heritage alive.

We continue past Petersburg,
entering North Carolina
through forested areas
and agricultural regions
growing cotton, peanuts and corn,
to Rocky Mount and Fayetteville.

Through darkened,
shadowed woodlands
surrounding the South Carolina towns
of Dillon, Florence and Kingstree.

Dawn's light frames a coral sky
above the large Atlantic seaport,
the beautifully preserved,
colonial city of Charleston,
on the Ashley and Cooper rivers.

We now follow the shoreline,
between marsh grasses, sanded banks,
tributaries, and small coastal islands,
to the towns of Yemassee and Beaufort.

Arriving in Georgia
at the graceful city of Savannah,
its National Historic Landmark District
personifies the feeling of the Deep South,
restored to its eighteenth-
and nineteenth-century elegance.

We proceed through dense pine forests
to the lumber and paper
manufacturing center of Jesup,
then enter areas of deep
vegetation, wooded tracts,
and tree-filled streams,
leading to the St. Marys River.

Florida north,
south through Jacksonville.
Lush, almost jungle landscape.
Palms in all sizes, varieties.
Heated crystal lakes boil
as the sun penetrates their silver,
to emerge from their silt-filled bowls.

Vivid equatorial flora,
colors intense,
reds, oranges, yellows.
Emerald, translucent, transparent.
Foliage embraces, intertwines,
enmeshes surrounding space.
Moisture, humidity, enables,
embodies plant life,
wild and cultivated.
Everything grows!

Spiderweb moss, Spanish ferns
sway from stately oaks,
filaments and strands
covering with a silken veil.

Across woodlands a pond lies
with cream-petaled
water lilies blooming
beneath heavily laden trees.

The South weaves its charm
over small towns and villages.
Brightly painted timber homes
with front porch chairs
well worn from rocking,
to the Lake George resort of Palatka.

Then through
De Land and Sanford,
the *Silver Meteor* arrives
at Winter Park's landscaped gardens.

A lone canoeist
on a sylvan lake.
Reflections, images of palms
shaped as cooling fans.
The forest floor now includes
spiky, prickly two-foot-high palms,
palmettos, amongst pine,
spruce and maple.

To Orlando,
major business center
with historic Old Town
and modern parks.
Here a magical theme land oasis
was built, in a place where,
fifty years past,
cattle and orange crops
were the mainstay,
and this unequaled dream
was as distant as the moon.

A compelling vision
of imagination took hold,
where visitors would assemble
to partake of, and participate in,
the show of shows.

A fantasy land was created
with replicas of nations,
of the Earth's near and distant continents,
bringing their heritage and customs.

Histories of communication
and future worlds explained.
Realms under the sea share their stories,
potential, their limitless possibilities.
Greenhouses where vegetables
of astonishing size
grow vertically to the sun.

From Orlando and Kissimmee,
landscape changes,
wild reeds and rushes,
elephant-like fronds appear.
Palms retreat,
and citrus groves
replace the pointed,
sword-like leaves.

Through Winter Haven,
land for travelers to the sunshine coast.
A retirement home from home.
Communities settle
in low-lying houses,
some on brick stilts,
some flat to the ground,
always earthed,
to Sebring.

Central Florida,
named for its rich flora,
retains its place of honor.

To Okeechobee, lakeside.
Wild waterfowl create
silhouetted shapes
through steep sun rays.

Towards the state's southern boundary,
entrusted to an aqua-turquoise pool
of outsize proportions.

The Atlantic shares its warmth
and terraced sands.
Resorts along the coast,
from the lustrous waters
of West Palm Beach, Delray Beach
to Deerfield Beach.

Southern palms attract
the northern spirit,
vacations, holidays,
beach goers, tourists.
Young and old
follow the mild shoreline
with enthusiastic fervor.

Population increases,
and in the growth the state prospers,
continues development.
Land reclaimed, skyscrapers built
to accommodate, fulfill
the needs of the coastal hub.

To Ft. Lauderdale
and Hollywood, Florida.
Water temperatures soar,
inviting, encouraging immersion,
the dip, the swim
in Nature's hot tub.

Industry of the sun,
baked at twenty-six
degrees north latitude,
the Golden City.
Restored Art Deco district,
atmospheric hotels and apartments
from the 1920's, in pinks,
lime greens, and turquoise.
The rhythms, the beat,
the southern tip of North America,
perched, poised to spread
hemispheric cultures,
the North to the South,
the South to the North,
Miami.

CITY OF NEW ORLEANS

From Chicago,
the night train to New Orleans
at Mardi Gras.
The atmosphere at Union Station, bustling.
Travelers arriving and departing
to and from long-distance destinations.

The *City of New Orleans* leaves
the cosmopolitan superstructures behind,
and voyages south,
past the residential
garden suburb of Homewood,
into rural Illinois.

Our journey takes us
through Kankakee and Gilman,
to the Champaign-Urbana campus
of the University of Illinois.

Streaming through
flat corn fields,
from our midnight window
moonlight touches
each frost-covered stalk
with an iridescent
and radiant glow.
Every plowed acre
becomes interwoven miles,
filling the nation,
and keeping the energy high.

We continue on through
agricultural lands,
widespread farms,
to the industrial cities
of Mattoon and Effingham,
towards the railroad town
of Centralia.

Past Carbondale's coal mining regions,
and crossing into densely wooded
areas of Kentucky, to Fulton,
we enter Tennessee on the approach
to Newbern and Dyersburg.

Nearing Memphis,
peach dawn reflects
on river streams.
Low-lying waters.
Cleared track through forest culture.

Delicate, white-steepled church,
narrow cone-shaped spire
above red brick.
Woodland turns
to small timber houses,
immediate response
to the urban development.

Roads become more frequent.
Ranch-style homes, terraced houses,
apartment complexes, duplex,
triplex, and a comfortable,
spreading population
with wide back yards,
one leading into the other.
Land to spare,
room for children to run.

The sun now climbs
over the horizon.
A bridge reflects its
simple concrete construction
in an adjacent pond.
The day has begun
and Memphis
turns out its night lights.

The city appears.
Hernando De Soto Bridge across the Mississippi.
Mud Island Exhibition Center,
storehouse of information
about the timeless river.
The Pyramid, amphitheater
for sports and musical events.
Beale Street and the Blues, inseparable.

St. Jude Children's Research Hospital,
untiring efforts to discover causes and cures.
Pilgrimages to "The King's" castle, Graceland.
Prestigious touring exhibitions
at the Memphis Cook Convention Center.
The Main Street Trolley.
The hundred-year-old Victorian Village,
opening its doors as a preserved monument.

From Memphis we enter
the neighboring state of Mississippi.
Small land holdings, isolated farm houses.
Corn and soy beans
live up to their full potential
on highly irrigated alluvial soil,
leading us to the heart of the Delta region.
The "Cotton Capital of the World,"
Greenwood.

Late February brings early spring
to Southern farmlands.
Tiny, tight buds
emerge on winter hedges,
to Yazoo City.

Standing water attracts wildfowl, geese.
River reeds fill shallow creek beds
as we continue through pine forests,
intermixed with hardwoods,
live oak and hickory.

To the state capital, Jackson,
on the Pearl River,
whose lumber, cotton and textiles
reflect Mississippi's major industries.

The *City of New Orleans*
arrives at Hazlehurst.
Timber fills freight cars in railroad sidings.
Lumber yards adjacent to the station
stack their boulevards of cut planks.
Box cars carrying fresh sawdust
stand clear, while logs piled high
are sprayed to retain moisture.

Forests of thick pine
are distanced by pastureland
immersed in deep meadow grasses.
To Brookhaven,
where prime Mississippi lumber
in tightly bound bales
again takes pride of place.

Through wooded,
unpopulated areas extending from
McComb, Mississippi.
Shapes to mesmerize,
to remake each spring.
Organic life hypnotizing
in its clean swept presence.
Timber reaching into sky space,
forming relationships of growth,
always in existence,
silent and articulate,
to Hammond, Louisiana.

The first Spanish moss appears
on tall cypress,
waving in mild winds,
decorating each tree.
Covering with draped
folds of soft shawls,
bringing a beautiful reminder,
the reality of a Southern past.

As we continue,
the moss thickens,
and trees become skeletal forms
in swamplands, bayou country.
Land forms not seen elsewhere, unknown.

Pelicans and ducks stand
on sand bars and upturned branches
in river tributaries.

Nearing New Orleans
we come to Lake Maurepas.
Lake Pontchartrain then
compels ours vision,
with shallow depth
and brackish waters,
salt from the Gulf of Mexico,
fresh from the Mississippi.

Here we find a way of life
adapted to the ebb and flow.
Houses raised high on stilts
on resilient mud,
above the water's reach.

From the train we see
the Louisiana Pontchartrain Causeway,
the over-water highway bridge,
twenty-four mile,
longest in the world.

We come to houses
adjacent to grass-covered mounds
higher than a rooftop,
the levee system
which encompasses the city.
Approaching the broad,
oval landmark, the Superdome,
we arrive at Union Passenger Terminal.

New Orleans fascinates
its people and its visitors,
drawn by the alluring attraction
of its world famous celebrations.
The winter Mardi Gras
and April Jazz Festival,
captivating the young and old.

French Louisiana
culminating in New Orleans.
City of suburbs, faubourgs,
stretching out from the original
French Quarter.
The influence, Creole, Cajun.
Exotic American center
of commerce and fashion.
"The Jazz Capital of the World."
The Mardi Gras Carnival
matching those of Venice, Italy,
and Rio de Janeiro.

America's sizzling
melting pot of cultures.
Gracious living.
Wrought iron balconies,
ladies strolling,
capturing the imagination.

New Orleans,
like New York, New Hampshire,
New London,
settlers in the New World,
bringing with them the cultures
of each source.

Louis XIV's Jewel of the Mississippi,
of the venture to America.
Fulfilling the needs of colonization,
business, and trade.
Forests adjoining,
protected by its sea walls,
and blending its tropical flora
with its lumber.

The "Crescent City," the essence,
pulsating, forming a resilient core,
focused at the fortified delta.
Retaining a spirit and flavor,
unique.

EMPIRE BUILDER

From Chicago, the central base
of America's railroad network,
the *Empire Builder* embarks
on its journey north and west.

Lake Michigan's deep turquoise presence,
endows the city with an invigorating
resource, giving vitality and a feeling
of lively well-being.

Chicago creates a balance
of metropolitan and cosmopolitan,
filled with fascinating history,
education, business, music, sports,
visual arts, theater, and natural beauty.
The world famous Art Institute of Chicago,
Museum of Science and Industry,
the Adler Planetarium,
the Chicago Symphony,
hot and cool jazz.

Every aspect
measures up to the heights
of its soaring landmarks,
the Sears Tower
and John Hancock Center.

Departing through
the commercial district,
the financial mecca
where skyscrapers
do reach the clouds,
the train passes through
industrial outskirts,
turning to low, leafy suburbs,
providing a continuity
to the great hub itself.

Then begins the transition
from highly populated settings,
through family farms
past Glenview, Illinois.
On entering Wisconsin,
the small, fertile fields become
widespread land holdings.

Crops planted
in soil of rich umber
tinged with charcoal.
Mineral composition, full-bodied.
Trees and shrubs,
awakening foliage
from a Northern winter.

Spring brings with it
a flow of gentle tones,
subtle movements
in the hue of the land.
Silver-green, emerald,
forming intricate mosaics,
frames of color,
independent yet reliant
on their neighbors.

Approaching Milwaukee
on the shores of Lake Michigan,
the radiating spires
of St. Stanislaus Cathedral
and the Basilica of St. Josaphat
stand out as we cross the Milwaukee
and Menomonee rivers.

We pass a memorable structure,
with three impressive glass domes,
the Mitchell Park Horticultural Conservatory.

Again into the countryside,
we encounter streams, tributaries,
at Okauchee,
opening onto Ocono Lake.

Timber-frame houses
share views of rowing boats
with people of all ages
fishing the clear waters.
The lake provides a focal point
for quiet settlement.
Peace in its surrounding beauty.

From Columbus, Wisconsin,
the occasional patch
of wild marshland
with ducks and waterfowl
becomes visible.
Emerging from a silent copse,
a tiny fawn looks
tentatively
at the giant train
as it journeys west
towards the Pacific.

To Portage,
sunset intensifies images
on evening waters.
Embankments support
a multitude of wildflowers
and spring growth.

We come to Wisconsin Dells station,
in the midst of spectacular lake scenery,
and pass through small towns
with houses from the turn of the century.
The land now changes.
Clustered rocks, hill formations
add diverse landmarks
to favored farmland.

As we climb more steeply,
trees now include spruce and fir.
Wild fuchsia and golden buds
brighten the edge of the track,
and dusk creates its special glow,
encompassing the train to Tomah.

Reaching La Crosse,
where the waters of the Black,
La Crosse, and Mississippi rivers merge,
we follow the route of the powerful
Mississippi, passing riverside towns,
leading to forests of oak and maple.
From our evening window,
we admire the beauty and sheer size
of the immense waterway,
as we proceed along its course.

During the night
the *Empire Builder* passes
Winona and Red Wing, Minnesota.
To the twin cities of Minneapolis-St. Paul.
This principal river port,
built in the early nineteenth century,
continues to bring prosperity to the region.

Through St. Cloud, Staples,
and moonlight over Detroit Lakes.

Entering North Dakota,
we glide through Fargo,
the state's largest city.

Six a.m. Grand Forks,
where the Red Lake River
and the Red River of the North unite.
Flat farmland, plowed.
Grain silos are filled to overflowing
with the mainstay
of this extensive farm belt.

Tree hedges are planted
to protect vast, open fields
from sharp winds and snows.
The elements reach out
to this widespread territory,
sustaining the land,
fulfilling its requirements
for strong winter wheat
and summer produce.

America's breadbasket.
Lands which feed the nation,
spreading for hundreds
of miles into the distance.

Approaching Devils Lake.
Significant flow, invigorating,
irrigating the plains lands.
Straw, reeds,
beige and golden,
border steel-blue pools
and marsh enclosures.

The North Dakota prairies
continue west,
through broad, grain-planted
fields to Rugby.

Passing cattle yards,
freight cars,
and locomotives,
the train stops at Minot.

The land now alters
to become gentle hills,
inland waterways,
lakes and pasture.

Oil wells dot the landscape to Stanley.
Plateaus, low, seasoned,
with mixed herds of cattle
walking beneath heavy,
rain-filled shadows.

To Williston,
Fort Union and Fort Burford,
we follow the shores
of the far-reaching Missouri River
into the expansive
wheat fields of Montana.

Arriving at Wolf Point,
small herds of goats
share the terrain
with horses wandering freely,
bays and golden palominos.

Striped farming,
honey beige and spring green,
to Glasgow, Montana,
geological storehouse
for fossils and dinosaur remains.

We pass Lake Bowdoin
National Wildlife Refuge.
Geese and ducks
with nests in high reaches.
Birds, wild and rare species,
perch protected, set apart to secure
the continuation of each special breed.

A heron is seen only from the train
as the *Empire Builder* continues
across northern Montana towards Malta,
Havre, and the Bear Paw Mountains.
These cone-shaped pyramids nearing Shelby
govern the surrounding landscape.

Then a land mass of proportions
great and nearly insurmountable.
From Cut Bank and Browning,
even in mid-May,
the peaks of the Rocky Mountains
in Glacier National Park
remain snow covered,
leaving no doubt
as to their majesty.

The train wends its way
closer to these towering summits,
and within moments
the scene is transformed.
Trees of evergreen,
mountains exquisitely drawn,
painted in stark black, grays and white,
with patterns etched of ancient frost,
molded and channeled
into the crevices
of volcanic upheavals.

To find the shortest route,
a scout must be sent
to explore and discover
on his own,
a needle's eye,
to enter and thread a track, a way,
clear, unequivocal.

Crossing through, cutting past
mammoth rock crags,
jagged intrusions into solid mass,
forming passages to break
the northern barrier.
To traverse across and between,
to attempt to reach the coastal plain
by sheer perseverance,
through a mountainous entry.

Ice sculptures,
multifaceted,
sharp crystal,
diamond clear,
priceless in their beauty.

Glacier National Park,
creations, formations,
from a time when worlds
were born.

A certainty
between these hallowed hills,
these monumental rocks,
connected and corrugated shields,
melded, welded together
by nature's hand.

Rising towards Marias Pass,
approaching the Continental Divide,
we reach Essex, where waterfalls
expand their territory,
tumbling, sparkling down steep inclines.
Firs and pines emerge.
The forested peaks
become clearly defined,
to West Glacier.

Night, the common denominator,
again restrains our vision
as we make our spirited ascent
through Whitefish and Libby, Montana,
across the border to the resort town
of Sandpoint, Idaho.

Crossing into the state of Washington,
we reach the vital city of Spokane,
and continue on to Ephrata,
in the Columbia River basin,
awakening in Wenatchee,
celebrated apple growing region.

This is a high country with
a soul, a spirit.
Living in the shadow
of the Cascade Mountains,
towns and villages, hamlets
are nestled beneath,
and surrounded by, dense forests
unchanged, untouched
in their natural beauty.

To Leavenworth,
with steep inclines
and breathtaking views,
the *Empire Builder* proceeds to Merrit,
and through the deep Cascade Tunnel.

We now encounter waterfalls
rushing down escarpments
of steep canyons.
Moss encrusted rocks allow
orange forest flowers to bud
from each crease and seam.

Change in foliage
at lower altitude,
nearing Skykomish,
gradient on the decline,
the train picks up speed.
We cross stream-filled valleys
tinted in dark plush greens,
as we make our descent
to the Puget Sound port of Everett.

The train glides
along the water's edge.
Steel-fresh air,
gulls dipping into the shallow banks.
Fishing boats make ready
to display the morning's catch,
to Edmonds.

Here ferries navigate in the Sound
to the Olympic Peninsula,
and distant outlines
of the Olympic Range
come into view.

Islands and islets
are immersed
in a pale-blue haze.
A rusted, sand-moored
ship bares its weathered hull.
Driftwood, drifting trees,
and planks of lumber
wash up on the nearby shore.
Vertical ferns mesh
with wild coastal foliage,
and we catch glimpses of geese
speeding across in search of food.

Yachts and trawlers
share harbor space.
Hillside homes are afforded
unobstructed views towards
Bainbridge and Whidbey islands
in the bay.

We approach
grain elevators,
cargo ships,
and freight depots
with freight cars
of northern railroads.

Waterfront wharfs,
container docks,
nostalgic streetcars,
and piers reconstructed
add to the atmosphere,
as we arrive at King Street Station,
in the Pacific Northwest's
dynamic seaport,
Seattle.

CALIFORNIA ZEPHYR

Late September, mid-afternoon,
leaving Chicago's
metropolitan Union Station,
its stately marble structure
reflecting the magnitude and character
of this leading Midwestern metropolitan city.
Chicago, center, point of departure,
catering for travelers on its giant rail network.

The *California Zephyr*
leaves the city on the lake,
through Naperville, and ventures
into the Illinois countryside.
Through rural farming communities
raising livestock and corn,
to Princeton and Galesburg.

Then crossing the Mississippi,
the dividing line,
from Illinois to Iowa.
Sunset creates reflections,
images, memories.
Remembering times past,
when river boats steamed north
and south upon these exalted waters,
these silted depths,
transporting prosperity
along its broadened shores.
Approaching the railroad town
of Burlington.

Heading due west, we continue at dusk
through plentiful Iowa farmland,
to Mount Pleasant.

From Ottumwa on the Des Moines River,
through corn country to Osceola and Creston,
we cruise immense grain producing areas
of the United States.

Crossing into Nebraska,
to the important cattle
and agricultural trading center, Omaha,
on the Missouri River.
We surge through acres, miles
of wheat and crops to be harvested,
to the state capital, Lincoln.

Passing Hastings,
the land transforms
from cultivated fields
to the grazing prairies
of the Great Plains.
Here we encounter the poignant site
of the Oregon Trail
on our route to Holdrege
and McCook, Nebraska.

Silver dawn unlocks the brilliance
of a Western sky,
as we enter Colorado,
arriving at Fort Morgan.

Soon the vaulted outlines
of a regal mountain chain
are seen on the horizon,
on our approach to Denver.
The Mile High City,
state capital of Colorado,
becomes a base for tourists
seeking the splendor
of this region.

From Denver
the *California Zephyr* climbs
with expansive views to plains
over the surrounding hundred miles,
as it maneuvers through the foothills
of the Rocky Mountains.

Past near vertical, tilted rock formations
standing guard over shallow valleys
of thickly planted fir and pine.

One rock becomes a landmark,
calling attention to its sculpted profile
formed as an elderly Native Chief,
keeping watch over the impressive
and spectacular terrain.

We weave through mountain passes
with views to Gross Dam Reservoir,
nestled high amongst these summits,
providing water to Denver's population.

Giant boulder canyons
grow ever steeper,
and peaks appear insurmountable
above valleys richly filled
with aspen of yellow bronze,
and spruce of deep forest green,
approaching Moffat Tunnel.

The train, through this
highest of passageways,
traverses the evocative
line of demarcation
of Eastern and Western rivers,
the Continental Divide.

To Fraser at Winter Park,
haven for travelers and skiers,
where waters, primeval lakes,
and sheer, translucent streams
add to the wonder of this tranquil
and inspiring setting.

Through quiet grasslands,
cattle-grazing pastures
climb onto clear ridges,
and plotted in the distance
are black and white herds,
to Granby, and the renowned
Rocky Mountain National Park.

Aspen are joined by evergreens,
and ground cover of sparkling-lemon
and alizarin-rose, along the banks
of September's Colorado River.

Leaves on the turn,
citrine, topaz, golden amber,
past crags and jutting, chiseled contours
becoming soft corrugated hills.
Rock skeletons are covered
in a finely woven fabric
of polished sand.
Wisps of late summer grasses
nurture the palomino,
chestnut, and dappled horses,
which thrive on this gentle range.

Harvest of colors,
outbursts, statements
to challenge the broadest of spectrums,
awaiting, anticipating
the oncoming of pristine white sheets
to be laid neatly
over rounded and upturned
angular forms.

New autumn winds through sun
give the appearance of summer,
then send waves
through tall mountain bush and flora.

In sheltered valleys,
one, two or three farms,
proudly decorated in glowing shades
of alpine wildflowers,
partake of the isolated existence.

Then, on pastureland
beyond Granby, not cattle,
but a prize, lone antelope
kneels in deep sagebrush.
Its gleaming antlers
attract recognition
in the cool afternoon light.

Wildlife, rare breeds
and well known,
are treasured gifts
in this high country,
seen from the moving window.

On entering Gore Canyon,
only the train passes
through its jagged walls,
so steep
that there is hardly room
to glimpse sunshine,
with edges so sharp
as if to cut paper,
all towering above
its breathtaking
white-water gorge.

Rapids, shimmering and effervescent,
rush with autumn fervor
as the Colorado cuts, steers
its way through the sand bed and boulders
of Little Gore Canyon.

Those who board the red and blue
canoes and rafts which attempt
its swirling currents, bracing themselves
for rides of stamina and courage,
will receive unequaled views upwards,
to the highest reaches
of these imposing, creviced cliff faces.
Their stature overwhelming,
like entrances to the great Pyramids.

These etched plateaus
now turn more and more
to coral-toned escarpments.
Circles of rock, globes of stone
on the tips of ancient cones.
Precarious positioning,
edge of precipice,
atoms of sand,
molecules in motion,
holding shapes and forms in place.

Sage, tumbleweed,
goldenrod, amidst amalgam,
full mineral content,
green copper ore,
red iron.
Geological surprises,
stirred to the boil
and melted down in layers,
stratifications,
some rounded, some serrated,
horizontal red-rock strata.

The river now crosses through
shallow beds, carved, incised.
Canyons are erased and eroded.
The process reduces the living land.

Momentum created
by the deeply moving,
ignited water base, forming gorges
and penetrated, engraved patterns,
digs at and into the earth,
until only particles remain,
to become passengers on the wind.

Gleaned and honed,
burnished and banished
into mighty air currents,
they are swooped down
and scooped up in a floating mist,
deposited with ferocious driving force
onto the river's glittering surface,
and into its transparent depths.

Two eagles
soar overhead
as the train climbs
within the tinted walls
of Red Canyon.
Rose and crimson shelves,
rust and vermilion,
swerve with a vaulting tilt.
Scarlet-veined layers above cream
cross the vision to Rancho Starvo.

Furrowed sands bask on silted banks
amidst hills and small farmlands
between Granby and Glenwood Springs.

Through mountain paddocks,
cattle thrive on late summer grasses
flowering upon
river-rounded stone hills,
when suddenly
Glenwood Canyon,
with its enormous,
asymmetrical, geometric surfaces
of fiery red magnitude,
overtakes the senses.

Upright and horizontal breaks.
The Earth's upper crust
thrown into open space
and left to land
unannounced,
in an unfamiliar location,
moving inch by inch,
layers continued
in new positions
of unaccustomed construction.

The train continues on,
through deeply etched ridges,
as passengers stare from the window,
in astonishment, dazzled.
Necks become craned
and gasps of awe
and admiration
are the only sounds
to be heard on our arrival
at Glenwood Springs, Colorado.

Then through the increasing
altitude of staggering
mountain precipices
and beyond, we enter
a changing landscape
of heat-scorched lands.

Cultivated only along
the Colorado's
fertile river basin,
they spread across
its broad flood plain,
with views
to Battlement Mesa's
extraordinary, high
earthen tablelands.

Far above sea level,
remainders, reminders
of an ancient geological past.
De Beque-Palisade leads
to the upper reaches
of Grand Valley,
and views to the famed
Grand Mesa, whose steep,
horizontal plane
is unrivaled in scale.
We now make our approach
past concave, convex,
undulating Book Cliffs,
to Grand Junction, Colorado.

From this scenic land,
where dinosaurs once ruled
with their imposing presence,
continue the monuments to color,
the outstretched,
carmine mesas bordering
the Colorado's vibrant-green
Fruita Loma Valley.

Again there is a change in temperature,
in elevation, as we rise through
the red rock of Ruby Canyon.
Monoliths worn
by a water's pressure,
a force so great
as to leave edges bared,
and spindles where once
were massive blocks.

These cliffs,
built of magnificent scarlet,
cubed and sphered,
boulder upon boulder
meeting at irregular junctures,
climb from the depths
of the ancient Colorado River,
with trees in clusters
along the river's edge.

The walls engulf our vision
in the warmth of hot-toned bedrock,
created when molten
mountains were plunged
into the depths of crevices
in the heated earth, and moisture welled
and vented forth into the atmosphere,
filling with gushing torrents
each formidable crack.

Then with a purpose so strong,
so compelling, that over millennia
as the waters bore deep,
the highlands became
low-lying integral plains.
The currents flowed and churned
until the jagged became softened,
the sharp became rounded,
and we could see
this powerful progression
in our moving observation.

The land now broadens, alters,
and becomes the dried, wide,
always envisaged,
always remembered,
authentic Wild West.

Sanded stone, crumbling rock,
exposed, unembellished,
vacant, bare, yet filled
with a permeating light,
creating mirages of imagination.

Brilliant, glistening waters,
nonexistent, appear salted
on the horizon.

Scorched, torrid
desert plains appear,
whose open boundaries
stretch to the distant mountains,
approaching Thompson, Utah.

Here we emerge at the gateway
to Utah's remarkable national parks.
Upturned, overturned
pink stone, forged and beveled
into rose-coral, carved,
precision-hewn formations,
by the great Colorado's
mighty hydraulic force.

Northern Utah,
shapes grazed, abraded,
worn with sand-blown winds.
Desert-heat induced,
unhumidified, solidified,
compromised by uncompromising
elements.

Along the Price River Valley,
a deer can be seen
feeding by the track,
but as we approach,
it rushes towards the nearby hills.

Here too, longhorned cattle graze,
and the land once more
provides sustenance,
to Helper.

Evening now descends
upon the train,
and through the night
we continue on to Provo,
then Salt Lake City.

On leaving this state capital,
echoes of the moon, stars, planets
vie for attention
in serene, midnight waters,
as we pass pools and outposts
of the Great Salt Lake.
To Elko, Nevada.

Sunrise, change of light.
Subtle contoured hills
and silk-like mountains.
Dawn's shadows
open and clarify
the morning's display.

Towns set on the flats,
soft, curving hills,
tactile, yet untouched.
The rails follow
their continuing course
to Winnemucca, Nevada.

Pointed reflections,
sun behind peaks makes forms sharp
to the eye, yet difficult to delineate.
The foreground is blurred,
the background, a tapering outline.

Silhouettes, striking,
silent and uncluttered,
simple and profound,
powerful to the touch.

Sands beneath sparse straw grasses
now become more outstretched, obvious.
Again the deserts descend
and the land drifts
with shifting motion.

Sagebrush clings tightly
to undetermined roots,
preparing for upheaval,
expecting to be uplifted
at any time.

And the burning, glowing star
pervades and perseveres,
forces its way across a cobalt sky.
Moves surely to penetrate
with its vibrant heat,
to soak up any moisture remaining,
turning the earth into dried fluid crystals.

From Lovelock,
sands have now taken over vast tracts,
with cactus buds the only enduring green.

Dunes rise and fall
in this landscape, unsheltered,
unprotected from heightened rays.

Shallow river bed
through sand-dune stark mountains,
to Sparks, Nevada.
Approaching Reno,
"The Biggest Little City in the World."

Suddenly the land assumes new dimensions.
Fir trees take the desert by surprise.
A watershed is found,
and as we surge upwards,
dry but fertile lands follow
in this spectacular terrain.

From Reno, the rise to cross
the Sierra Nevada Range.
Forging through mountain ridges,
sculpting tunnels from formidable rock,
and into steepest cliff sides.
To create a passage, the track builders
of the mid-nineteenth century
invented a railed pathway
through age-old stone.

Constructing with feats
of skill and human power,
breaking their way through,
to transport us over and above
our expectations.

Equaling the treeline,
beyond the craggy, rock-faced ledges.
This metallic, sinewy, wavy line,
where cloud cover becomes enmeshed
with stone, where solid matter
and vapor become one impenetrable mass,
and we, as travelers,
glide through and become one
with the beauty of this scene.

We follow the boulder-filled
Truckee River basin,
in the Tahoe National Forest,
to Truckee, California.

Nearing Squaw Valley,
the train enters a horseshoe turn
through Coldstream Canyon.
We then climb through summits
layered with lodge pole
and Jeffrey pine, white birch,
spruce and cedar.

To Donner Pass,
above crystal-blue-turquoise Donner Lake,
site, one hundred and fifty years ago,
of early pioneers trapped
by a severe Sierra Nevada winter.

We enter covered snow sheds,
protecting trains from mountain blizzards,
allowing passage through the buildup
of snow, rocks, trees and ice,
to Lake Spalding.

The feeling of the Gold Rush
still lingers, with images of wagons,
of prospectors and pioneers
breaking their way through and across
steep canyons and ravines,

changes in climate and landscape,
in the often elusive search
for a precious yellow metal.

The ore which brought a population
to Immigrant Gap and Gold Run.
From the steep ridge above Bear River,
they dismantled wagons
and carried their belongings
through rugged Bear Canyon,
to eventually reach the American River,
near Sutters Mill,
site of the first gold strike.

The *California Zephyr* now descends
through rolling foothills
to the towns of Dutch Flat and Colfax.
Born of the mining fever,
the passion which settled
California's north,
to Roseville, then Sacramento,
establishing this great city
as the state capital.

Our course alters once more,
as we sweep through
broad agricultural lands, to Davis.

To Suisun City and Fairfield,
past trading ports along
the water's edge.
Martinez on the shores of Suisun Bay,
to Richmond, Emeryville,
and our final destination, Oakland.

Deep harbors, moorings, jetties, wharfs,
all storing and transporting huge cargoes
in container vessels, oil tankers, barges
navigating the commanding body of water,
San Francisco Bay.

SOUTHWEST CHIEF

The *Southwest Chief*
makes its night departure
from Los Angeles,
stopping at the California cities
of Fullerton, San Bernardino,
Victorville, Barstow
and Needles.

Awakening between Kingman
and Flagstaff, Arizona.
Clouds of peach crimson
blend and mesh,
as dawn permeates
with fire in the sky
above dark silhouettes
of volcanic mountains.

There is no mist
enshrouding this rugged chain,
and every sharp outline
burns its way upon our sphere
of vision.

The sun breaks
into existence
with no hesitation,
and in the clarity
of its strength,
colors are heightened
and defined.

Sagebrush covers
iron-oxide earth,
and open range turns to forests
of ponderosa pine
on hill country,
as far as the eye
can see.

Heading east, the land
becomes more mountainous.
The train enters into hillsides,
carves its route through a carpet
of deep-maroon soil,
as it follows upwards
on a slower gradient,
through woodland camps.

The steeper the climb,
the higher the spruce and pine become,
with the occasional passage
revealing green, plush-textured,
then ivory-tipped
summits in the distance.

Herds of wild deer
graze near the track, offering a view
of the natural world rarely glimpsed,
but through the windows
of our moving carrier.

Climbing towards Flagstaff,
we see volcanic upheavals
of sixty million years.
These now softened, silver-green hills,
born of molten cinder-cone eruptions,
stand next to, and ready to defend,
their mountain kin,
the snow-covered
San Francisco Peaks.

From Flagstaff,
the land suddenly declines,
descends into even, horizontal prairies,
becomes parched with the sun's
penetrating rays, and is again
concealed by dry desert sagebrush.

Enriched colors
of mineral rock
rebound against canyon walls.
Rounded conical structures —
not striking peaks —
subdued by time, leveled,
until finally dissolving
into flattened arches,
straight to the distant
horizon.

Drained of moisture,
crags appear where
rivers once flowed.
Dried, silted boundaries
forming miniature
Grand Canyons.

Cattle feed on sparse grasses.
Unannounced, unexpected,
clumps, mounds
of auburn fragments,
globular and oval,
as if spread
by a giant's hand,
cover the thirst-felt earth.

Soil becomes soft
and sandy,
few plant species
daring to break through.
The broad desert opens
its enormous shell,
its clay pearls
glisten in the light
of early morning.

Low-lying plateaus
come into view.
Strange table shapes, sliced,
flat-topped, crew-cut,
some with spherical boulders,
some jagged,
unapproachable.

Distant headlands,
individually molded in fluid stone,
create a backdrop
for an unpaved
drive-in theater
nearing Winslow.
A town engulfed in tumbleweed
so thick, so full, that if it ceased
to exist, the dried, rolling growth
would overtake and overrun
development.

Following on,
we pass trading posts
displaying Native American crafts
of the Southwest.
Vital reservoirs
provide water
for local cultivation.

Evergreen shrubs,
remaining emerald
even in the soaring heat,
complement pink-tinged
desert bushes,
whose brilliant shades
enlighten the subdued,
subtle tones of the drylands.

Russet-shale stone formations,
even-layered mesa plains,
fired and dried.
Mud flats, creased and cracked,
become etched patterns
on the searing,
hardened earth.

With quiet caution,
antelope enter this heated realm,
feeding on wisps of golden stalks,
wild oat, barley, flax.
Arid grazing land
shared with cattle
in small herds.

The train winds smoothly
through stratified,
marbled rock forms
which remain
unchanged, untouched
in their breathtaking power.

Scattered wooden corrals
and windmills are juxtaposed
against hot-coral cliffs.
Crumbling edges of broad,
dried river crossings
are eroded into sand-filled banks.

Uplifted flatlands
amidst desert juniper
provide a sun-bronzed home
to gleaming horses,
roaming without boundaries.

At the Arizona-New Mexico border,
approaching Gallup,
the wild rock formations
turn from sand-beige
to red-rust
in Red Cliff country.

Appearing as giant, washed,
beached pebbles at the entrances
to unexplored caves,
monumental cliffs,
rich in the glow of brick-dust
and burnt-orange strata,
begin to cast their spell
over the surrounding landscape.

Shapes suggesting
architectural images stand out.
Pyramid Peak, Church Rock,
hewn from flame-toned mesas
one hundred million years past,
as the inland sea
of western New Mexico
receded inch by inch.

Clouds create patterns
on these hot-carmine banks.
Rooftops of tiled dwellings,
adobe construction
of clay and straw,
are brushed with crisp,
snow-like sand crystals.

Clay, terra-cotta-caked river beds
and escarpments sketched
in weathered, crimson stone,
shaded with iron-rich oxidation,
produce startling contours
against a transparent azure sky.

Ancient black lava in rugged mounds
stretches for miles,
following straight, flowing lines
parallel to the track.
Ravens soar, casting shadows
over fractured remains, ruins,
in twelfth-century rendered stone
of the Anasazi people,
to Albuquerque.

Here in the valley
of the Rio Grande we find a city
of industry and commerce.
Home to Native American tribes,
where, on the station platform,
gifted artisans sell crafted wares
in traditional designs,
sharing with travelers
the history of each piece.

A Navajo story-telling doll
in ancestral dress.
Jewelry of Zuni and Navajo
sterling silver,
coral and turquoise,
rings, bracelets and beads.
Coyote and bear earrings,
and a pendant formed as a legendary
feathered dream-catcher.

Beyond Albuquerque
we pass its celebrated landmark,
Sandia Peak.
At sunset, the steep, polished cliffs
turn to luminescent coral,
deep watermelon color.
Its tramway to the top
transports visitors
to unparalleled views
of the surrounding plains.

To Lamy, New Mexico,
gateway to sixteenth-century
Santa Fe, state capital
and acclaimed artistic center.
Through Apache Canyon,
whose narrowest access
to Glorieta Pass
creates a jagged tunnel
from which the train
steadily climbs, then descends
into sparsely cultivated
red-rock desert.

Throughout this dry river valley,
mesa plateaus take precedence.
These ancient, raised seabeds,
smooth, bald-topped,
jut from the earth
and oversee vast stretches
of cattle country.

Inorganic mineral features,
products of a cataclysmic age,
when wild nature,
unquenched natural forces,
unleashed with burning power,
moved and motivated
a young, molten Earth.

At times plunged beneath steep oceans,
at times uplifted into fiery heats,
these now cooled, quieted forms,
mellowed and unadorned,

provide an arid focal point,
a stark and poignant memory
to fill our spirits with awe,
as the *Southwest Chief*
cruises alone, amidst
the splendor of this scene.

Herds in this land of baked earth
need all allotted grazing
to sustain nourishment
from scarce, parched grasses.

Further on,
Shoemaker Canyon
is home to wild deer
on plains lands outside
Shoemaker Pass,
feeding in small groups
on sun-sealed pastures.

Occasional houses stand out,
built in traditional New Mexican style.
Adobe with rounded corners,
light caramel
or raw sienna in color,
flat roofed for dry days
and cool desert nights.

The train now passes through
the Santa Fe National Forest,
with piñon pine, tamarind trees,
and herds of white-tailed antelope.
To canyons, layered, broken into
cubes of rock, tons in weight,
some of which cannot withstand
gravity's continuous pull,
and shatter as they tumble
to the earth below.

Approaching Las Vegas, New Mexico,
the air fills with deep violet,
shades of mauve converge,
as we wind further
into the torrid highlands.

Without warning,
at mid-afternoon,
vertical streaks
of silver lightning
extend downward
into an ever darkening sky.

Dividing, separating
the atmosphere in two
with their sheer will.
One half lapis, ultramarine-steel,
the other, quicksilver,
fluid mercury.

Arrows from the moon,
metallic rods piercing the dusk light.
Fragmented meteors, streams,
showers of glass,
crystal spears.

The afternoon sky becomes yet more
primed for the ensuing torrent.
Storms become apparent,
water sheets can be seen
to the far distance and beyond.

The first drops
drift across the windows
of the *Southwest Chief.*
Day appears night,
and the earth of this open plain
which has been calling out in thirst
is now quenched, filled.
This grazing, broad
pasture will again
provide for its herds.

Sun to the far west
now brings clarity to the open vista.
As instantly as it began,
the rain has passed,
a prairie storm
realizing its swift
and powerful destiny.

To Raton, New Mexico.
Through its pass,
looking towards its summit,
Raton Tunnel, above
seven thousand feet,
becomes the highest point
on the train's ascending route.

Cattle range on low pastures
by the dry river canyons
of hundred-year-old
Dick Wootten Ranch,
built along the historic
Santa Fe Trail.

Arriving in Trinidad, Colorado,
late dusk, magnificent
Fisher's Peak rises high over this,
the largest town since Albuquerque.

Extraordinary mountains
of the Culebra Range
reach their flat-topped pinnacle,
towering over the rising streets.
Adjoining land is cultivated with
terraced hill slopes, broad open country
spreading into the distance.

Soon darkness affirms its dominion,
and the train continues on through Colorado,
to La Junta and Lamar.

Through the night we pass
Garden City, Kansas,
and the legendary towns
of Dodge City and Cimmarron,
recalling memories of the building
of the American West.

The coming of the railroad
brought settlers to these extensive plains.
Farmers and herdsmen,
wheat and cattle, to the towns
of Hutchinson and Newton.

Onwards we pass through Emporia
to the Kansas state capital of Topeka,
arriving at dawn in Lawrence.

We awaken
to the sight of luxurious green
farmland and forests.
Not dry, spacious prairies,
but soft, rolling country
with well-manicured fields and crops.

America's heartland,
central to its core.

Timber merchants,
lumber yards.
Acres planted, filled
to their chlorophylled brims,
to the outskirts
of Kansas City, Missouri.
Magnet to railroads
and modern business center
within this important
agricultural region.

Heading east we find
an outstretched canvas
of dazzling pinks, reds and violets,
flower producing areas,
fields in cultivation,
to Marceline.

Huge stretches of farmland
become one region
and reason for existence,
landscapes made for
and nurtured by the plow,

accepting and thriving
on the responsibility
to produce and supply.
To fulfill the vital link
in the food chain.

From La Plata, Missouri,
to the early Iowa settlement
of Fort Madison.
We span the river crossing,
banks deep red-umber in color,
the immense propelling waterway,
the currents of the Mississippi.

An expansive vista now unfolds.
The river's power to provide
is utilized, through its branches,
for miles,
towards Galesburg, Illinois.

Farms merge,
creating a textured fabric
of green and gold,
with the occasional town
scattered between
more open country,
to Princeton.

Passing the outlying
residential suburb of Naperville,
foundries, refineries,
machine shops,
and railroad yards
lead to the nucleus,
point of concentration,
hub of Midwestern culture,
Chicago.

DESERT WIND

Leaving the "City of Our Lady
Queen of the Angels,"
Los Angeles.
Business center of the Southwest.
Hollywood,
where the world looks
to fulfill its dreams.
The film industry in all its glory,
movie and television studios,
homes of the Stars.

City whose outstretched panorama
spreads to a culture
built in the open air.
Los Angeles,
warm and temperate,
world famous theme parks,
beaches from Long Beach, Redondo,
Santa Monica to Malibu.

Outdoor concerts
at the Hollywood Bowl,
stage productions
at the Greek Theater.
The Music Center of Los Angeles,
Mann's Chinese Theater,
the Los Angeles County Museum of Art,
the Museum of Contemporary Art,
historic Olivera Street,
the J. Paul Getty Museum,
the Huntington Library
and Collection.

Los Angeles attracts,
as if with gravitational force,
and with its growth,
outwards and upwards,
its cultural presence
also expands.

Mid-morning,
the *Desert Wind*
embarks on its way
through palm-filled
industrial sites
where bougainvillea
creates magenta, orange
and white displays
on subdued stucco factory walls.

Greater Los Angeles
spreads its population
at low-level throughout
its extended basin.
Industry is replaced by
single-story suburbs,
shopping malls,
school bus depots,
swimming pools,
willows, and tropical ferns.
The city merges with its neighbors.

To Fullerton, where
the land is surrounded
by steep escarpments,
sun parched cliffs,
rising above golf courses,
and homes roofed
in warm, muted
terra-cotta tiles.

To San Bernardino's
Spanish-style station,
towards the town's
namesaked mountains.
We now commence
the impressive climb
through the horseshoe curve
and steep grades of Cajon Pass.

Views are ever present
over the outspread
metropolitan area,
through yellow-cut stone,
and past the rare,
magnificent forms
of Joshua trees
in the foreground,
to Victorville.

We now reach the railroad
junction town of Barstow.
Its history as a Santa Fe Trail
way station brings visitors
seeking the essence
of a Western past.

Then rising from
the steaming terrain,
small oases.
Sagebrush in clusters,
and gilt-copper
sculpted mountains
in the distance.
Eroded undersea gateways
to the depths of worlds
unfathomed,
thrust upon high ground.

Over land,
under sea-blue skies.
Majestic, heat waved,
baked, broiled.
Colors undiscovered,
rose green, lime rust,
mauve beige,
subaquatic hues,
overturned, fine-tuned,
highly flammable,
hot!
Sand particles descend,
dusting, smoothing down,
rolling with fragments
of parched earth.

A windmill creates power
for one lone homestead
surrounded by dune-laden
lava hills,
ancient marine eruptions,
mineral-fawn before violet-gray
sheets of crisp shale,
powdered,
sand encrusted.

Hedges, bush, and wild flora
are covered with fine layers
of wind-borne silt,
blown through waterless nights
when small desert creatures
open their eyes
and venture out
from the safety
of their cool abodes
into the world of sustenance.

In this land
beyond sagebrush
and sand layers,
tiny palms appear
before triangular mountains.

The American West
in all its splendor.

Joshua tree forests,
each tree an individual,
all related, members
of the same family,
yet differing,
widely varied in form.

The train continues
through open, unpopulated expanses,
and sands caressed by sun-dried grasses
sweep the vista, as we approach
the Jewel of the Mojave Desert,
The Great Oasis,
Las Vegas.

Electric incandescence.
Center of a monetary universe.
A fantasy land
from an arid dream,
amidst wild nature's backdrop,
with mountains underplayed
by the world's largest
man-made luminous star.

A realm of Egyptian Pharaohs
and Roman Gods.
Of a circus spectacle
and King Arthur's Court.
Of a Hollywood showcase,
buried treasure, and a raging volcano.
Of an interior rain forest
and a railroad station casino.
Of cowboys, showgirls,
unlimited themes and electricity.
Where day and night share
the same persona,
and hours blend,
becoming one another.

Following the dazzling luster
of Las Vegas,
the train passes through
dried river beds
and bleached canyons
of subtle, sunset colors.
A light which permeates
and pervades, casts
each pebble and grain
with a rose-golden glow.

The buildup of tiny
grass fronds streaked
with platinum
makes a lasting,

though fleeting,
impression on our senses,
like glints and glimmer
of a topaz-sequined robe
covering the expansive vista,
as the sun plays
with patterns created
by its light.

Silhouettes, shadows
of free standing pillars,
dusky monoliths fuse
as evening overtakes the *Wind*
on its midnight route
through Caliente, Nevada,
and Milford, Utah,
to Salt Lake City.

Arriving moments
before dawn embraces
this valley setting,
between the stately
Oquirrh Mountains to the west,
and to the east, the imposing peaks
of the Wasatch Range.

Distinctive outlines of the city
come to light.
The six elegant towers
of its esteemed place of worship
in Temple Square
soar upwards.
The copper dome
of the state Capitol,
built in polished
marble and granite,
creates an august presence
amidst the natural wonders
of the Great Salt Lake.

CAPITOL

The local train, the *Capitol*,
travels through Berkeley
towards Sacramento.
A new carriage glides,
elegant, tranquil, subdued
in color and decor.

The San Francisco hills
become ever more prominent,
growing in stature
as we weave our course
northward.

Sand dunes, dusted mounds,
particles of rock,
joined, clinging one
to the other,
form shallow, undulating,
shaded banks.
White herons in groups
settle into grassy marshlands.

The open sea broadens
across the bay.
Moss covered rocks
and shapely stones
are uncovered
by the evening tide.

A lone fisherman
stands chest high in cold
northern California waters.
The penetrating chill
does not deter his quest.

Small craft are harbor-moored,
while ducks, green iridescent crowns
glistening as they emerge
from silted depths,
search for shelled food.

Sailing boats navigate
through sheltered coves
and inlets
beneath an industrial backdrop.
White sails, with red numbers
showing their positions
in the evening's race,
place them in good company.

As they pass,
swelled by the motion
of the breeze and currents,
cane sugar factory buildings
and trees bent by salt winds
and shaped into horseshoe
sculptures
become their
points of reference.

As the light of dusk
lowers in intensity,
a disused dock
creates charcoaled
silhouettes and patterns,
like a city of ancient
timber skyscrapers
fulfilling their mysterious
destinies.

The train winds
along the coast,
in amongst boulders,
plants and bushes
betrothed to the sea,
configurations melted
and molded
by inconspicuous
eons of time.

Salt shadows glimmer,
forming memories
on the horizon.

Heavy steel bridges,
heroes in their strength,
built to last
upon monumental supports,
span a waterway which evokes
a feeling of magic
when spoken,
the bay of San Francisco.

To Martinez.
Distant foothills are carpeted
with sun-baked grasses,
ripened-wheat in color.
Bushes thrive,
succulent, replete
with desert fruits.

Changes in humidity, temperature
come early to the northern
California coast.
Heat waves,
drying ocean marshes,
country soil prepares
for deep summer.

Coconut palms stand firm
alongside willows.
Cedars and poplars
provide cover
in back gardens
bordering the track.
Cone-shaped evergreens,
from an Italian landscape,
furnish nesting space
for migrating sea birds.

Hills of beige velvet,
and silken bushes
of deep forest green
connect to form
a continuous border
on the distant rise.

Ranches of cattle,
and fields, furrowed
and corrugated
by the plow,
await the season's harvest.

Entering the central plains,
evening-deep
mauves and pewters
take precedence,
filling our range of vision.
Rising slopes,
steep inclines,
become opaque contours.

The sun remains west
behind crinkle-cut hillsides,
forming a shimmering presence,
straight and horizontal
across the deepening sky.

No translucent vermilion
sunset today.
Instead, it is
serene silver platinum,
tinged with lemon gold.

Duck-egg blue sweeps
a cream-satin streak
across the purple horizon.

A glow of honeyed silk
engulfs a mare
and chestnut foal
as it prances,
brushing gently
against its mother.
This evening's silent brilliance
highlights the newborn's
exquisite and delicate form.

All of nature
becomes magically transformed
in this light,
as the train makes its way
through fields, open
and ready to produce
in abundance.

Every bush,
bale of hay,
broad-faced sunflower
has a special strength,
beauty.
Day is ending,
evening is on the wane,
but the glorious sun
bestows one final grace
upon the Earth
before it is compelled
to give way,
to take its leave
from the pretender
to the throne of night.

And we are allowed to watch,
to see, to take part,
to participate
in the light show.

We are allowed to share
the subtle tones,
the gleam through
haze-borne clouds,
sterling and powder-blue,
broken, shattered by
the penetration of light.

The sun refuses to depart
without one ultimate,
earth-shaking,
searing flood of power,
breaking through,
discoloring reflections,
altering perceptions
and identities.

Decreasing color,
manufacturing a broader spectrum,
imitating a paintbrush
with no primary colors.
Reinventing the limited palette,
with one, and only one,
golden-peach scepter
on the horizon line.

Even white, wild blossoms
do not know their names,
their hues.
They are lost
in the colorless shade,
abandoned by
our friendly star
for the duration
of the uncompromising,
moonless night.

To Sacramento.

COAST STARLIGHT

Leaving Seattle, Washington,
on the *Coast Starlight*,
the world-famous Space Needle
makes its indelible imprint,
towering above
the high-rising offices
and hillside homes
of this Pacific Northwest
city with an upbeat.

Harbor life along
the Puget Sound's
ferry wharf beams
with a continual flow,
transporting passengers
to adjoining island shores.

The specialized market
at Pike Place
shares the old and new,
antique and ultramodern.
Foods of all varieties,
descriptions are found here,
fresh fish and produce
abundantly arrayed.

Brave and hardy settlers
of the nineteenth century
who made the perilous
northern crossing
are remembered
in Pioneer Square.
The City of the Underground
creates its spellbinding presence,
as this municipality continues
to grow and prosper
into the new millennium.

Heading south
we pass King Dome Stadium,
and perceive the distant, bold outlines
of the Olympic Mountains
standing regally above
a fertile landscape.

From the shoreline,
the metallic, gleaming
islands of Puget Sound
come into view,
creating silver images
of lace-patterned trees
upon these enigmatic waters.

Small farming communities
dwell amidst plowed clearings,
interspersed with golden
Scottish broom.

Further on we pass towns
where every home has a garden
and every garden is pruned
and kept within its crafted perimeters,
leading to nearby meadows
and golf courses.
Here in November, full-flowing,
gushing rivers surge through
the Washington countryside.

Fields are saturated,
rivers reach their brims,
autumn colors capture
and captivate the vision,
and crops develop and thrive
in this irrigated landscape,
lush with vegetation.

Rhododendrons bring
wild-fire color
to the surrounding scene.
All growth is unstoppable,
like a cool jungle
ripe with pink
chestnut buds
and azalea bushes,
of colors so bright
as to appear artificial,
not nature made.

The combination of mists
and the richest of soils
produces a cultivated
rain forest of overwhelming
beauty.

Wildflowers in bright magenta,
white and brilliant yellow
verge upon the track.
Forest parklands
and hillside suburbs,
mining explorations
and factories are followed
by boat-mooring jetties.

Lumber yards are filled
with cut timber planks,
local forests yielding
their generous harvests.

Valley farms
with grain silos
and crimson barns
take, keep hold
of the countryside,
until we reach
the city of Tacoma,
its wooden houses,
neatly painted
in pastel shades.

Major shipyards
engaging ongoing
activity of a working harbor.
Ocean-going cargo vessels
and small pleasure craft
are afforded views of the hilled city.

Passing this leading port,
south from Seattle,
the waters of Puget Sound
are seen for mile upon mile
along the railroad's
western border.
Ancient pilings and docks
remain as landmarked
reflections in deep pewter.

Popular restaurants and homes,
built on a water base,
claim their territory
along the shoreline
of Commencement Bay.

Geese, pelicans, egrets
and sea gulls perch high
on disused moorings,
searching the depths
for their swift-moving prey.

Spruce and poplar intermingle
as the track climbs
above the sheer,
tree-laden embankment.

Forest farms, green velvet moss,
lichen-encrusted bark,
and golden meadow grasses
adorn the cliff stones
along this narrow ledge,
until the waters
of Puget Sound disappear
from view.

To Olympia-Lacey station
at Olympia, state capital
of Washington.

Moving steadily,
we pass barns of chrome red
built along the Skookumchuck River.
Nurseries of pine seedlings
growing in gradations,
regenerating and replenishing,
continue the tradition
of woodland renewal, to Centralia.

Recent rains have brought
forth a multitude of waterfalls,
cascades which reach and fill
the Cowlitz River and its tributaries
to their uppermost limits,
just resisting the desire
to overflow their banks
onto neighboring fields.

White corral fences
protect their horses,
as farms continue to spread
to the borders
of Kelso-Longview.

Trees growing right out
of rocks alongside
the track are bound
by white daisies
and woven mosses.

The train heading inland
through broad valley farms
follows the shores
of Lake Vancouver
to Vancouver, Washington,
the Pacific Northwest's
oldest settlement,
endowed with a deep
natural bay.

We cross the Columbia
then Willamette rivers,
with traffic carrying
cargo of all dimensions.
Deep freighters, primed in red ocher,
black and white, or steel-blue-gray,
ship vast containered weight,
bulked goods, to all
industrial ports and corners.

From this point,
the broad Columbia River
becomes the dividing line,
the flowing boundary
between Washington state
and Oregon.

To Union Station, Portland,
principal harbor
on the Columbia's southern shore.
"The City of Roses,"
parks and gardens,
flourishes within the lush forests
of its surrounding countryside,
ample rainfall encouraging
vibrant growth.

From Portland,
through the Willamette Valley's
farms and fir plantations.
Crops of spinach and kale
thrive under clouds
of heavy-blue-charcoal
highlighted with
cobalt patches.

Passing Aurora,
with views to Mt. St. Helens
and majestic Mt. Hood.
Pastures and agricultural lands
are ever present,
to the rich fruit bowl
of Gervais.

Here grow fields of irises
in shades of cream,
lemon yellow, peach,
white with deep purple,
and intense orchid blue.

Through Woodburn,
with houses in striking
turquoise and primrose.

Cattle wander under a sky
promising imminent storms.
Clouds alternate
over this fertile land,
fluctuating from heavy
iron grays
to intermittent azure,
allowing gentle, clear
windows in the storm
to tantalize distant
mountain peaks.

A Northwest autumn sky.
Shades of dove
and polished granite
spreading for miles
above small towns.
Children in yellow school buses
are returning to their homes
as the train approaches Salem,
with its impressive
marble-built state Capitol.

On leaving
this prominent city
we pass a llama farm,
home to rare breeds,
and a single deer
feeding amongst
a large herd of sheep,

keeping grasses
cropped and cut,
in this flourishing valley
bordered by the Willamette River.

Small hamlets settle beneath
rounded soft peaks,
with crested trees rising towards
shadowed embankments,
to Albany.

Passing Three Sisters Mountains
to Eugene, Oregon,
the land flattens.
Farms are ever present,
with paddocks,
apple orchards,
evergreen nurseries.

Lumber yards
and A-frame homes
stand out along the banks
of the Willamette,
as the train enters Oakridge,
distinguished by its unique landmark,
the beautifully preserved,
red-painted covered bridge.

This small country town,
residing within an emerald,
gently sloping valley,
becomes the point of departure,
the base from which we commence
our ascent into the Cascade Range.

The valley falls
under the spell
of November mists
and the deep glow
of massive firs.

A vista now opens up
above the fog cover.
The distant outline
of soaring Cascade Summit
can just be seen
as snow and cloud
converge, blending
into and beyond
the horizon.

As we climb further
through the mountains,
snow falls.
Mammoth trees now tremble
under the weight
of their gentle captor.

Pink-amber needles
at the base of mighty pines
catch the brilliance,
diffusing the bright reflection
of light confronting our vision.

In these high altitudes,
conifer forests spread
as far as the eye can see,
planted in chestnut,
deep mineral-fed earth,
dusted with a fine coating
of frozen liquid crystals.

Climbing steadily,
snow covers rocks and fissures.
Mid-November, southern Oregon
awakens to the chill.
Fallen logs produce
shadowed patterns,
juxtaposed
one upon the other,
in the untouched, frosted layer.

To Diamond Lake and Chemult,
ripe russets, burgundies,
cadmium orange,
raw and burnt sienna.
Autumn foliage
beneath steep hillsides.

Slender trunks of silver birch
stand out against
the spruce, pine, fir
and mountain laurel
which cover
this expansive range.

Falling snow clings
to frozen summits,
building layer upon layer
its crystal bright cover,
transforming bald, sharpened ridges
into white down blankets
covering glacial cradles.

Sunset now extends
over the alpine landscape.
Golden streaks grow
into platinum, glowing strands
highlighting silhouettes
of distant mountains
and autumn-bare twigs
and branches,
to Upper Klamath Lake,
Mt. McLoughlin
and Klamath Falls, Oregon.

Here, in the glow of dusk,
we find transparent, still
green waters, faint ripples
of a gentle undercurrent,
rolling motion
against a steep backdrop.

Only conquests of Space
can compare
to this craggy canyon view,
sometimes engulfed,
embraced by fog-mists,
open to the train alone
as it pursues its goal,
its quest, its need
to overcome geography
and the elements.

Formidable task,
uncompromising effort,
colossal monument
to human endurance
and invention.

Conifers, evergreens,
from seedlings to eighty-foot,
mighty, mature trees,
stand tall on steep
mountain inclines,
as the train quietly,
smoothly enters each curve,
rocks with each railed movement
shaped in stone one hundred years past.

Caressing the continual edges,
embracing the contoured cliffs,
the train commandeers its space,
its own iron pathway,
hewn out of solid mass,
into the valley below.

And where no routes
could follow,
tunnels were engineered
through the mountain depths
allowing the train's
positive passage.

Evening becomes clear night.
Mountain shadows
shape their infinite realms,
and the *Coast Starlight*
forges, maneuvers
the curving bends,
as throughout the night
it climbs onwards
through the Cascade Range.

Passing the glowing outlines
of snow-capped Mt. Shasta,
above the northern California
town of Dunsmuir.
To scenic Redding,
by the shores of Lake Shasta,
we near the entrance
to the Great Central Valley,
arriving at the fruit growing
agricultural centers
of Chico and Marysville.

Houses then take
the place
of conifers,
stucco replaces timber
construction,
and as we reach
the state capital,
Sacramento,
the population
of this great state
makes its presence
known.

Through palm trees
and spruce,
the gilded dome
of the Capitol
comes into view.

Sacramento,
born when California's gold
was king.
When prospectors came
by horse, on foot,
and by the wagon load,
building a city
whose wealth now derives
from the rich harvests
of its valley farms.
The California State
Railroad Museum
brings to life the heritage
of a railroad past.

Emergence of light
as we cross the Sacramento River,
to the university town of Davis,
passing mountains and rolling hills
towards the port of Martinez.

Across San Pablo Bay,
from Richmond and Emeryville,
we become transfixed
by the magical skyline
of San Francisco.

The glittering city
which captures the imagination
of tourists the world over,
and of local residents
eager to sing its praises.

Seen from the *Coast Starlight*,
the bay of San Francisco
opens deep and wide.
The Oakland Bay
and the Golden Gate bridges
span and connect
this magnificent waterway.

As we approach
this city of pearls,
unmistakable cable cars,
commerce, modern architecture,
banking empires founded
in the rush for California gold,
we find a strength
and diversity of cultures,
old and new inhabitants,
all combining to create its
fascinating atmosphere.

Music in the streets,
open-air museums,
richly planted public gardens,
all aspects becoming
one cohesive and vibrant whole,
in a setting of harbor wharfs,
bays and inlets.

Freighters, tankers,
yachts and cruising vessels.
Fishing boats sell their precious cargo
fresh to the stands and restaurants
awaiting the crowds at world famous
Fisherman's Wharf.

To Oakland,
with its newly built station,
spacious and light,
to accommodate passengers
traveling north, south,
and across the bay.

As we depart, we pass
the bustling plaza
of Jack London Square.
Through docks,
mechanical cranes, containers,
and salt-flat marshlands.

To the gateway of the computer
empires of Silicon Valley,
at San Jose.

Here we encounter
one of the twenty-one
California missions founded
by Father Junipero Serra
along the eighteenth-century
El Camino Real,
"The Royal Highway."

Heading southwards
into the Santa Clara Valley,
agriculture begins once more.
Produce of all descriptions
is cultivated here.
We see flower farms
and deep-orange
pumpkin fields.

Eucalyptus and Christmas trees
grow beneath a setting of soft,
ocher, rolling hills,
accentuated by yellow blossoms,
leading to the Santa Cruz Mountains.

To Gilroy,
"Garlic Capital of the World,"
with its renovated Spanish church,
and fields upon fields
of this healthy, flavorful
plant.

Through Elkhorn Slough,
protected nesting ground
for wild waterfowl,
with water entering
from exquisite
Monterey Bay.

We enter Pajaro Gap,
where the train seems almost
close enough to brush
against the walls
of this sun-baked canyon,
on its route to Watsonville Junction.

Here, spreading for miles,
are strawberry
and lettuce fields,
spinach and chard,
apple orchards.

The *Starlight* continues on
to Castroville,
"Artichoke Capital of the World."
Acre upon acre, row upon row
of full, ripening artichokes,
moist with spray mist irrigation,
planted in the deep
raw-umber earth.

Agriculture expands
in every direction.
Red foxes dressed
in winter camouflage
of dark beige
rush across open fields.
Marshland, flat reed canals
provide habitats
for sandpipers and herons.

Approaching John Steinbeck's
ancestral home, Salinas,
whose valley known
as "America's Salad Bowl"
forms the vast vegetable garden
of northern California,
bordered by oranges in groves
and willows' sweeping branches.

Beneath the Santa Lucia
and Diablo Mountain ranges,
enormous farm tracts,
spreading southward,
lead to the arched, vaulted
Santa Clara Range,
above sweet-water,
sun-bleached straw.

Familiar crops of potatoes,
corn, and the succulent,
blue-toned leaves of cabbage.
Lettuce bursts forth in a multitude
of sizes and varieties,
in deep reds and olives.

In neighboring fields,
broccoli, kale,
mustard greens, radishes,
and tomatoes ripening
sustain health-giving growth.

Now vineyards commence their reign
over allotted space,
interspersed with rows,
straight and long,
of cauliflower, onions and carrots
in traditional formation,
growing in profusion.

The California sun
creates its miracle,
entices tiny shoots
out of the rich earth
at great speed,
provides its nurturing
warmth, encouraging
all forms of vegetation.

Golden-winged hawks, blackbirds
and flocks of gulls flutter,
hovering over newly planted tracts
in search of nourishment.

Yellow plows work and connect
these unlimited fields,
acres wide.
Some remain cleared,
awaiting planting,
while others show off
their new growth, grain specks
in the distance, which
within days will proclaim
their chosen forms.

A national, natural
treasure chest, brimming over.
Its bounty bridging
the Great Divide,
encompassing boundaries,
to be shipped to the East,
North and South.

As the Salinas Valley ends,
another area, rich in minerals, begins.
Oil wells spread
their strong cast-iron forms
across the landscape.

River streams and tributaries
provide needed water
for steeply sloping pastures,
historic sheep-grazing lands
of Basque herdsmen.

We pass the missions
of Soledad and King City,
then ruins of eighteenth-century
Mission San Miguel,
whose intriguing gate
and shallow walls remain
within its creviced perimeters.

Laurel and ash line communities,
houses with paddocks,
horse corrals, stables,
in open-riding grange country.

To Paso Robles,
"The Path of the Oaks,"
central California wine country,
vineyards rising in production.
Sun reserved, revered crops.

From Santa Margarita,
the *Coast Starlight*
climbs onwards through
November-dried summits,
golden straw in color
and texture.
Seasonal rains
not yet quenching the thirst
of this mountainous terrain.

"Our Lord's Candle" yucca,
with voluminous
white-cream blossoms.
Wild mustard, lupine,
Canadian crystal,
wild turkey,
turkey vulture,
deer and goats
each take their place
in this remarkable landscape,
as the train
continues south
over the Cuesta Grade,
prized landmark
of this central region.

We now cross
Stenner Creek Trestle
and into two one-hundred-
and-eighty-degree horseshoe curves,
bringing the surrounding peaks
within our vantage point.
A vision of the Seven Sisters
comes into view,
San Luis Obispo's majestic
mountain chain of volcanic elevations,
sculpted into pinnacles of beauty.

From this tranquil
mission town,
hills have a softened character,
each in harmony
with the other.

Harvest colors,
subdued and subtle.
Straw, olive, muscatel,
mauves and golds,
with red-rust berries,
adding shaded texture
to the sun-warmed
agricultural lands.

Past a memorable rock formation
resembling the face of a man,
honored in times past
by Native American tribes.

To shadowed inclines,
where ancient rivers
forged their way
through hillside stream beds,
causing the sandy stone
to form stalagmite
and stalactite shapes.
Dried, eroded, parched canyons,
ridged gorges emerge.

Corrals in valleys
with winds from the sea
offer training grounds
for thoroughbreds,
as golden-feathered hawks
circle.

Plant life changes
to sea flora.
Low-lying bushes and shrubs
cluster on sandy soil,
growing full in protective
cover.

First sighting,
unsurpassed,
of the majestic Pacific Ocean,
companion to the *Coast Starlight*
for over one hundred miles
south to Ventura.

From deep, foam-filled crests
along the contour
of the shore,
terns and herons seek out
elusive shell fish,
while gulls and pelicans
soar above the afternoon waves.

Then passing through
broad expanses
of Vandenburg Air Force Base.
The site of Minuteman,
Titan 2, and Peacekeeper missiles
creates its own
distinctive landscape,
with launching pad towers
in deep contrast
to earlier cities and forests.

From Surf,
throughout this immense area,
sea plants remain
close to the earth.
Shielded against ocean winds,
petals in lemon yellow,
fuchsia, orchid and lavender
cover moisture-filled
ground roots.

Australian eucalyptus
thrives along California's
western border.

Vineyards plentiful,
grapes ripe, smooth to the touch.
The coastline shimmers
as if through desert heat.

To Point Honda,
southwards through Point Arguello,
known as the Graveyard
of the Pacific.
Rocky ledges
jutting into the ocean,
at times submerged in deep fog,
have in the past
claimed lives and vessels.

Towards Point Concepcion,
between San Luis Obispo
and Santa Barbara,
sloping grassy canyons
lead into the sea.
Succulent plants spread
to sun-tanned cliffs,
bluffs encrusted
in silken Pacific sands.

The coast's wild presence
is seen, as cypress windbreaks
mold to the wind's direction.

The Santa Ynez Mountains,
furrowed, undulating,
descend to meet the train.
Herds of cattle graze
on inner hillsides
beneath juniper and myrtle.

To El Capitan State Beach,
set in quiet coves
below sea-worn cliffs.

Black-ash-fertilized lands.
Ponds abundant
with small sea birds
approaching
Gaviota State Beach,
where surfers and sea gulls
share territory.
Flocks of California
Brown Pelicans flying south.
Noble birds
with broad wing spans,
keeping in single-file formation
above the central California
coastline.

The occasional
fishing boat
and cruiser float
on afternoon still waters.
Eucalyptus, palm and pine
appear on the approach
to Refugio State Beach.
Its quiet bay gives
tranquil refuge amongst
sheltered rocks.

Sea birds gather,
searching in the cool
shore sands,
for crab, muscle and clam,
intent and intense
as the train passes
without disturbing
their concentrated effort.

To Tajiguas Creek Trestle,
bridge above the ocean,
track set between
surf and mountains,
closest to the water's edge.

Waves break and recede,
lines diminish.
Fine and sharp crevices
in sea-sculpted stone
combine with driftwood cities
to adorn secluded beaches.

Ferns, pampas grass and pasture land
lie close to the track above the sea,
as the *Coast Starlight* arrives
at Goleta.

The train rushes between shoreline
and the ever-steepening mountains
approaching Santa Barbara.
These grow in stature,
forming an imposing background
to this elegant city,
one of California's
highlight coastal towns.

A garden community,
overflowing with bougainvillea,
clipped and manicured hedges,
lilac jacaranda, willows,
tall and slender coconut palms.

At the station stands
a magnificent Moreton Bay fig tree,
which for over one hundred years
has spread its asymmetrical
branches, hovering, covering,
providing shade and shelter.

On the outskirts south,
we travel alongside
the Andree Clark Bird Refuge,
lake and bird sanctuary
of the Santa Barbara
Zoological Gardens.

This noted wildlife preserve
attracts rare and endangered species
to its waters and islands.

We now resume our course
past ocean and shore,
houses and boulders.
Coastline homes
with panoramic views
are hidden beside the track,
until again
it is only the Pacific
and the train,
on the edge
of the Western World.

On clear, open beaches,
surfers await
the "Big Wave,"
while companions watch
from the shoreline.

Afternoon sunlight,
deeply slanted,
rose bronze and copper orange,
a setting sun of extravagant hue.

We stream through
citrus groves, newly planted,
lettuce and corn.
Then wind-swept cypress,
driftwood in clusters,
carved, molded,
formed on the beige
and stone-speckled shore.

At sunset,
hundreds of blackbirds
swirl, spiral
in clockwise formation,
directly above
the surf at Ventura.
Strays penetrate
the vortex.

Islands
in the Santa Barbara Channel
are highlighted
by a cinnamon sky.
Warm spice reflections
on cool California waters
become unchallenged
lightning streaks,
with newborn stars
connecting,
forming images,
above the charcoal evening's
steel, stone
departure.

Night cloaks the train
in deep violet
on its southerly course.
Traveling inland, we pass
Oxnard's modern station,
and the stately mission church
at Camarillo.
Through Moorpark and Simi Valley
to Santa Susana Pass,
its gold-tinted boulders
in fascinating,
stacked formations,
to Chatsworth.

Into the San Fernando Valley,
to Van Nuys,
geometric patterns of light
engage our vision.
Television and film studios appear
on our approach to Burbank.

Through the residential
streets of Glendale,
and along the Los Angeles River,
we come to the final destination
of the *Coast Starlight*,
the beautifully restored,
Spanish-style Union Station,
Los Angeles.